The Purpose-Driven Leader

Navigating Ethical Challenges in a
Goal-Obsessed World

By Mike T. Lightner

Chief Master Sergeant (Retired), US Air Force

D2D
DARE2DREAM
LEADERSHIP DEVELOPMENT

Alaska

Printed in the United States of America

First Printing, 2026

ISBN-13:
Paperback: 979-8-9932603-0-3
Hardcover: 979-8-9932603-1-0

Dare2Dream LD Productions
dare2dreamleadership@gmail.com

www.d2dleadership.com

Table of Contents

Foreword

During my career, I have frequently been asked, "Why professional ethics?" – why break out this field of ethics for special attention? My reply was – and is – that professional ethics by its very nature involves identifying and prioritizing values and courses of action that call for moral responsibility, individual and organizational *conscience*. Professional ethics is not about *espoused values* – it is about *values-in-action*. And professional leadership – if it is to be leadership with integrity – needs to appreciate the central *threat* to individual and organizational conscience.

That threat is teleopathy,* the unbalanced pursuit of goals due to fixation, rationalization, and (eventually) detachment. This phenomenon has been observed in business, law, medicine, space exploration, sports administration, and even forest firefighting. It has been called "channelized attention" in fighter pilot training, and "reckless summit fever" in mountain climbing. My guess is that the narrowing of goals (fixation) is a phenomenon that can be found in most, if not all professions and occupations – and that the *antidote* of moral responsibility or conscience is therefore relevant at every turn.

Mike Lightner offers in *The Purpose-Driven Leader* an insightful and practical book on this subject, especially in the business arena – the threat to individual and corporate conscience. He offers "real stories" and "practical tools" to address the challenges of teleopathy presented in those stories. In my experience, this is the approach of case method pedagogy. But in this book, case examination is enhanced. Lightner "zooms out" after "zooming in" by raising deeper "Pause and Reflect" questions and inviting readers to develop "Visions for Change" to shape a better future for businesses and other institutions.

The measure of an effective teacher is his or her ability to foster not only knowledge *about* a subject but the *appropriation of that knowledge* for use in the learner's own environment. This calls for Socratic questioning, the kind of questioning that elicits self-awareness on the part of the person(s) being questioned. Lightner shows in this book that he is such an effective teacher.

In a polarized world, it is not narrow ideological thinking that is needed, but instead comprehensive moral thinking. *The Purpose-Driven Leader: Navigating Ethical Challenges*

in a Goal-Obsessed World is a refreshing example of just the kind of thinking we need.

-- Kenneth E. Goodpaster, Professor Emeritus
University of St. Thomas, Minnesota

*From: teleo (in Greek meaning "goal, target") and pathos (meaning "sickness, disease.")

4

Dedication

To Professor Kenneth E. Goodpaster,

This book would not exist without your pioneering scholarship and generous mentorship. Your groundbreaking work on teleopathy—particularly your seminal articles and book chapters that first defined this concept as the "unbalanced pursuit of goals"—provided the intellectual foundation upon which the entire manuscript is built. The clarity, moral insight, and ethical rigor of your writing shaped every chapter, from the initial exploration of teleopathy's symptoms to the practical frameworks for overcoming its destructive effects.

Your willingness to engage with a former military enlisted man and aspiring author, offering encouragement, thoughtful feedback, and unwavering support, inspired me to transform a college paper into this book. Your example of scholarly integrity and commitment to ethical leadership has been a guiding light throughout this journey.

With deep respect, gratitude, and admiration,

Mike T. Lightner

Author's Preface

The thoughts, lessons, and stories in this book have been decades in the making. It started as a brief observation but then grew into something much greater...a deep-seated desire for understanding. You see, in the very early part of my military career, I had noticed that leadership would release policies, programs and/or incentives with what I believed to be the greatest of intentions. However, when the policy, program, and/or incentive was put in place at the lowest level, it would oftentimes have a countering effect. Meaning, things would get worse and not better.

For example, when I was in the 43rd Tactical Fighter Squadron in late 1988, we had a shop policy which allowed us to have off every other Friday during the summer, if our work was done by close of business Thursday. For our shop, this worked great. Everyone understood exactly what needed to be done and we did it. Our shop was amazingly clean, our people were well trained, and our equipment was perfect.

There were four of us working in the shop at the time and it seemed like frequently three of us would be off fishing one Friday while the other would stay back to answer the phones. The next week, three of us would be working while the one who previously stayed behind, would go and do whatever it was she did on her days off. This worked perfectly for us, productivity, quality, and morale were extremely high.

However, it didn't seem to work like that for everyone.

There was another shop in the same building as us who also had four people working in it. When they heard what we were doing they decided to do it as well. Unfortunately, this policy had a negative impact for them. Their equipment quality went down, their shop was a mess, and they started to fight over whose turn it was to take the day off. After a few months, their shop chief stopped the program, and they went back to everyone working five days a week.

At the time, I thought that was interesting, but I was still new to the Air Force and really didn't think on it very long. Then, as my career progressed, I started seeing similar examples over and over again. The people changed, the locations changed, even the type of work changed but the one thing that didn't change was people taking what was intended to be something good and somehow twisting it into something bad. I couldn't even tell you how much money I've seen wasted by people doing the craziest things to make numbers on a chart look good, only to turn around and do it again next week so that leadership wouldn't figure out what was truly broken or that they lacked the parts needed to do things correctly. This is teleopathy in action—obsessing over a goal (like time off or making numbers look good) without balancing the ethics and long-term impact.

In this book, I will share with you much of what I've learned as well as many stories to demonstrate what I had seen. I'll also include some well-known stories from history and maybe even a few hypothetical ones just to spice things up a bit. My goal is for you to learn from my experience, so that you don't get caught up in the seemingly never-ending cycle of seemingly positive intent, followed by negative unintended consequences.

Introduction: The Ethical Edge in Leadership

Imagine you're a young executive, burning with ambition. Your company's stock is climbing, your team's hitting every target, and the board is singing your praises. You're on fire, chasing that next big win—a promotion, a record quarter, a legacy-defining deal. But one day, you wake up to headlines screaming scandal. Your team cut corners, ignored red flags, and betrayed trust, all to meet those goals you set. The fallout is brutal: customers leave, employees quit, and your reputation lies in tatters. What went wrong? You didn't just miss a target—you fell into the trap of *teleopathy.*

I'm Mike Lightner, and I've seen this trap up close. As an Air Force Retired Chief Master Sergeant with over thirty years of service, I've led teams under pressure, where the mission was everything. But I learned early on that chasing goals without a moral compass can lead to disaster. Years ago, I watched a colleague push his unit to hit impossible deadlines, ignoring safety protocols to "get it done." The result? A costly mistake that grounded our operations and shook our team's trust. That moment stuck with me, inspiring me to dig into why good people make bad ethical choices. The answer? Teleopathy—a term coined by Professor Kenneth Goodpaster, describing the unbalanced pursuit of

11

goals that blinds us to what's right. In his latest book, Times of Insight, Professor Goodpaster equates this to a similar hazard taught to military fighter pilots called channelized attention.

Channelized attention is defined as the severe narrowing of focus onto a single, specific task or piece of information, to the point where other critical, peripheral, or situational cues are ignored. Often referred to as target fixation or cognitive tunnel vision, this phenomenon is a significant human performance limitation that can cause a dangerous reduction in overall situational awareness.

Although channelized attention is something somewhat unique to military fighter pilots, executing complex maneuvers at extremely high speeds, Teleopathy can be experienced anywhere from the boardroom to the flight line and even within your family at home.

Teleopathy isn't just a fancy word; it's a leadership killer. It's what drove Enron's executives to cook the books, chasing wealth while betraying employees and investors. It's what pushed NASA to ignore safety warnings, leading to the tragic Columbia disaster. And it's what tempts leaders every day to prioritize profits, deadlines, or status over integrity. In today's world, where headlines scream of corporate scandals—think Volkswagen's emissions fraud or Wells Fargo's fake accounts— teleopathy is a threat we can't ignore.

THE PURPOSE-DRIVEN LEADER

But here's the good news: You can lead differently. Ethical leadership isn't just about avoiding scandals; it's your competitive edge. When you lead with integrity, you build teams that trust you, customers who stay loyal, and a legacy that lasts. This book is your guide to spotting teleopathy, breaking its grip, and leading with purpose. Whether you're a CEO, a manager, or an employee dreaming of making a difference, these pages will equip you with tools to navigate the ethical challenges of a goal-obsessed world.

Why This Matters

Let's get real: The workplace is a pressure cooker. Deadlines loom, shareholders demand results, and competition never sleeps. It's easy to get tunnel vision, to chase that next win at any cost. But when you do, you risk losing sight of the people who matter—your team, your customers, your community. Teleopathy creeps in when you're so focused on a goal that you forget your values. It's like driving with blinders on, speeding toward a cliff while ignoring the warning signs.

I wrote this book because I believe leaders can do better. While working on a college paper on teleopathy my eyes were opened to how good intentions can go wrong when goals take over. Drawing on real stories—like Enron's collapse and NASA's tragic mistakes—this book will show you how teleopathy undermines ethics and what you can do about it. We'll explore practical frameworks, from stakeholder theory to ethical principles like care, virtue, and duty, to help you lead with productive harmony. And we'll dive into real-world examples, from Nike's labor controversies to Patagonia's ethical triumphs, to inspire you to make a difference.

What You'll Discover

This book is divided into 11 chapters, each packed with stories, insights, and action steps to help you lead ethically. Here's what you can expect:

> **Real Stories**: From Enron's fall to Patagonia's rise, we'll unpack true stories of teleopathy and ethical leadership.

> **Practical Tools**: Each chapter offers "Leadership Action Steps" to help you apply what you learn, from stakeholder analyses to ethics charters.

> **Reflective Moments**: "Pause and Reflect" questions will challenge you to think deeply about your leadership and values.

> **A Vision for Change**: We'll look at how technology, global perspectives, and ethical frameworks can shape a better future for business.

Leadership isn't about hitting every target; it's about hitting the right ones. By the end of this book, you'll know how to spot teleopathy, avoid its pitfalls, and lead with a conscience that inspires others. Let's get started on your journey to becoming an ethical leader who changes the game.

Pause and Reflect

- What's one goal you've chased that caused you to overlook something important? How did it affect your team?

- How can leading with integrity give you an edge in your workplace?

Leadership Action Steps

1. **Define Your Values**: Write down three core values that guide your leadership. Check if your current goals align with them.

2. **Start a Leadership Journal**: Keep a notebook to track decisions where ethics and goals collide. Review it weekly to spot patterns.

Chapter 1: The Trap of Teleopathy: When Goals Blind You

Let me tell you a story about a company that had it all—bright leaders, big dreams, and a skyrocketing stock price. Enron, in the late 1990s, was the darling of Wall Street. Executives like Ken Lay and Jeff Skilling were hailed as visionaries, transforming a humble gas-pipeline company into a global powerhouse. They chased ambitious goals: dominate energy markets, innovate trading, and make shareholders rich. But behind the scenes, something was wrong. They were so obsessed with profits that they cooked the books, hid debts, and betrayed everyone who trusted them. When Enron collapsed in 2001, it wasn't just a company that failed—it was a wake-up call for leaders everywhere. Enron's story isn't just about greed; it's about *teleopathy*, the leadership trap that blinds you to ethics when you're chasing a goal.

I've seen this trap in action. In my Air Force days, I worked with a superintendent who was laser-focused on mission success and believed everyone was as focused as he was. Because of this he trusted those below him to do their jobs without proper oversight, ignoring warnings about equipment serviceability. One day, during a Higher Headquarters (HHQ) inspection, the entire program imploded, nearly grounding our operations, which would have cost millions of dollars. He wasn't a bad person; he was just caught in Teleopathy's grip, so focused on the mission and his beliefs that he forgot the people and principles that made it matter. That's what this chapter is about: understanding teleopathy and how it turns good leaders into cautionary tales.

A few years after retiring from the Air Force, I got a job as the Director of the Anchorage Small Business Development Center (SBDC). During the hiring process, I learned that the SBDC was created to help reduce the number of small businesses that failed in the first five years of operation. During the interview, they said all the right things. But when I started to dig into the job, I found they were doing nothing to resolve the original problem. Instead, they were hyper-focused on pushing business loans. Why, because this was the easiest matrix for them to track in order to secure future funding from the Small Business Administration. Six months into the job, I resigned. Within a few months of my resignation, my entire team had resigned. Why, Teleopathy had taken hold, and everyone could see it but the leadership.

What Is Teleopathy?

Teleopathy, a term from Professor Kenneth Goodpaster, is like a fever that takes over when you chase a goal too hard. It's the unbalanced pursuit of one objective—profit, deadlines, success—to the point where you ignore everything else, like ethics, people, or long-term consequences. Think of it as goal sickness. In business, it's what happens when a leader says, "Just hit the numbers," and forgets to ask, "At what cost?"

Great leaders don't just set goals; they balance them with conscience. Enron's leaders didn't. They had a Code of Ethics—Ken Lay even sent a memo in 2000, preaching respect, integrity, and excellence. But their obsession with wealth drowned out those words. They used shady accounting tricks to inflate profits, ignoring employees, investors, and customers. The result? A $74 billion collapse, thousands of jobs lost, and pensions wiped out. Enron shows us that teleopathy isn't just a personal failing—it's a leadership disaster that hurts everyone.

The Leadership Lesson

Why does teleopathy matter? Because every leader faces pressure to deliver. Maybe you're chasing sales targets, project deadlines, or a promotion. It's easy to get tunnel vision, to think, "If I just hit this goal, everything will be fine." But that's where teleopathy sneaks in. It whispers, "The end justifies the means," and before you know it, you're compromising values you swore you'd uphold.

Take a moment to think about your own leadership. Have you ever pushed your team so hard to meet a goal that you overlooked their well-being? Or justified a shortcut because "it's what the boss wants"? Teleopathy doesn't just happen to CEOs; it can strike anyone who loses sight of the bigger picture. The good news? You can avoid it by leading with balance, keeping your eyes on both the goal and the people it affects.

The Stakeholder Connection

One way to beat teleopathy is to embrace stakeholder theory, a principle that says leaders must serve everyone their decisions touch—employees, customers, suppliers, shareholders, and communities. Don Mayer, a business scholar, puts it this way: Leadership isn't about picking one winner; it's about balancing competing interests. Enron's leaders forgot this. They chased shareholder value but ignored employees who lost their savings and customers who trusted their energy services. The result was a failure no one could ignore.

To further see how teleopathy undermines the stakeholder connection in practice, consider the real-world case of the Schlitz Brewing Company in the 1970s. At the time, Schlitz was America's second-largest beer producer, trailing only Anheuser-Busch. Under CEO Robert A. Uihlein Jr., the company was obsessed with reclaiming the top spot and boosting profits. Facing rising costs and fierce competition, executives pursued aggressive cost-cutting as their primary goal, rationalizing changes that compromised product quality.

They shortened fermentation time from over 30 days to as little as 15, replaced expensive barley malt with cheaper corn syrup, and added a foaming agent to mask the thinner taste. These shortcuts saved money short-term, but the beer became cloudy, less flavorful, and prone to spoilage. Customers noticed immediately—complaints surged, and in 1976, Schlitz had to recall over 10 million bottles. Sales plummeted, but instead of acknowledging the quality issues, the CEO and leadership rationalized the decline. They blamed changing consumer tastes, market saturation, and tough competition, insisting the cost reductions were necessary for profitability in a difficult economy. This detachment from reality ignored clear evidence from customer feedback and internal warnings.

The rationalization exemplified teleopathy's symptoms: fixation on profit goals blinded them to ethical risks, rationalization excused shortcuts, and detachment from stakeholders led to betrayal. Customers, the primary stakeholders, were sold an inferior product, eroding trust and driving them to competitors like Budweiser. Employees faced the fallout—layoffs and morale hits as the company spiraled. Shareholders saw the brand's value drop dramatically, culminating in Schlitz's eventual acquisition by another brewery. Even the community suffered, as Milwaukee felt the economic hit from the company's decline.

This case highlights why the stakeholder model is essential to combat teleopathy: leaders must balance goals with the needs of all stakeholders, not just shareholders. Schlitz's failure breached duty ethics by ignoring obligations to deliver quality and virtue ethics by lacking honesty and courage to admit mistakes, as we'll discuss in Chapter 3. Later, we'll see how frameworks like Professor Goodpaster's perspective-frankness-engagement approach could have prevented this—by engaging stakeholders early and being frank about risks.

The Schlitz story isn't isolated; it echoes Enron's executives rationalizing fraud to meet financial targets or Volkswagen's emissions scandal, where goals trumped ethics. When leaders rationalize unethical practices to hit numbers, they disconnect from stakeholders, inviting disaster. As we'll see in subsequent chapters, breaking this cycle starts with recognizing teleopathy and reconnecting with those who depend on your decisions.

Breaking the Trap

Teleopathy is a trap, but it's not inescapable. I've watched good leaders fall into it and even better ones climb out. The ones who escape do so by refusing to treat goals as sacred. They ask the tough questions early and often: "Is this goal worth the cost?" "Who gets hurt if I push too hard?" "Am I staying true to my values?" "What are we missing here?" These aren't soft questions—they're the hard edges that keep you from sliding into the abyss.

In the military, I've seen this play out time and time again. Units chase impossible readiness numbers or deployment quotas, only to end up with safety violations, burned-out Airmen, and equipment that failed when it mattered most. The leaders who broke the pattern weren't the ones who lowered standards; they were the ones who raised their eyes and asked whether the target was still the right one. When the answer was no, they adjusted— sometimes at personal cost, but always with the mission and people in mind.

The same dynamic plays out in business every day. A sales leader pressures the team to close deals at any cost, and suddenly corners get cut, truth gets bent, and trust erodes. A CEO obsesses over quarterly earnings, and quality suffers, suppliers get squeezed, employees burn out. The trap feels productive at first—numbers look great, bonuses flow—but the damage accumulates quietly until it explodes in negative press, lawsuits, lost customers, or a team that no longer believes in the mission.

Great leaders break the trap by remembering that goals exist to serve something larger: the people they lead, the customers they serve, the values they claim to uphold. They build in checkpoints— regular moments to step back and evaluate not just what they're achieving, but how they're achieving it. They surround themselves with people willing to speak uncomfortable truths. And they accept that sometimes the bravest decision is to slow down, rethink, or even establish a new path to the goal when the original path has gone off course. Remember, the goal isn't what is important, the purpose of the goal is what truly matters.

In the chapters ahead, we'll go deeper. We'll examine teleopathy's three core symptoms—fixation, rationalization, and detachment—and how they quietly poison decisions (Chapter 2). We'll look at ethical frameworks that act as guardrails, pulling you back when the pressure mounts (Chapter 3). We'll walk through real-world stories of leaders who fell in and those who climbed out, so you can recognize the warning signs in your own organization (Chapters 4–6). And we'll equip you with practical tools—checklists, decision templates, team exercises—to make ethical leadership routine rather than reactive (Chapters 7–9) and we'll apply these lessons to modern challenges like DEI/ESG, showing how polarization amplifies teleopathy. (Chapter 11).

For now, hold onto this: Leadership isn't about hitting every target. It's about hitting the right ones—the ones that make your team stronger, your organization healthier, and the world a little less cynical. When you chase goals without asking the hard questions, you risk becoming the very leader you swore you'd never be. But when you lead with purpose, with an eye on stakeholders and values, you build something that lasts.

The trap is real. The way out is simpler than most people think: stop running long enough to look up, look around, and make sure where you're going is still where you want to end up.

Pause and Reflect

- Have you ever seen a leader so focused on a goal they lost sight of what's right? What happened?

- What's one area in your work where you might be at risk of "goal sickness"?

Leadership Action Steps

1. **Map Your Stakeholders**: List everyone affected by your current goals—team, customers, community—and assess how your decisions impact them.

2. **Check Your Goals**: Schedule a monthly review to ensure your goals align with your core values. If they don't, adjust course.

Chapter 2: Spotting the Signs: Fixation, Rationalization, Detachment

Picture this: It's February 1, 2003, and the space shuttle *Columbia* is soaring back to Earth after a successful mission. The crew of seven astronauts is ready to come home, and NASA's team is buzzing with pride. But something's wrong. As the shuttle re-enters the atmosphere, it disintegrates, leaving a nation in shock and seven families in grief. The cause? Not just a piece of foam hitting the wing, but a leadership failure rooted in teleopathy. NASA's obsession with meeting a tight launch schedule blinded them to safety warnings, costing lives and billions. This tragedy, like so many others, wasn't about bad people—it was about good people caught in teleopathy's grip, showing symptoms that every leader needs to recognize.

In my Air Force days, I saw these symptoms up close. A Maintenance Officer in the 90th Fighter Squadron (FS) at Elmendorf Air Force Base (AFB), let's call him Captain Tom, was a rising star, driven to get our unit's aircraft back in the sky after maintenance, in order to meet our Wing's Aircraft Utilization Rate (hours per aircraft per month) goals. He pushed the team relentlessly, ignoring mechanics' concerns about rushed repairs and moving parts from flyable aircraft in order to fix aircraft that hadn't flown in the past few weeks.

One day, while swapping the landing gear from one aircraft to another, mistakes were made and a part was damaged. The results, two broken aircraft both left without usable landing gear. Captain Tom wasn't evil; he was just fixated on the goal, rationalizing shortcuts, unnecessary maintenance practices and detached from his team's warnings. That's teleopathy at work, and it's why this chapter is critical. To lead with integrity, you need to spot teleopathy's three warning signs—fixation, rationalization, and detachment—and stop them before they derail your leadership.

The Three Symptoms of Teleopathy

Teleopathy, as Professor Goodpaster describes, is like a virus that infects your leadership when you chase goals too hard. It shows up in three ways: fixation, rationalization, and detachment. Think of them as red flags waving in your face, warning you to slow down and check your compass. Let's break them down, one by one, with stories that hit home and lessons that stick.

Fixation: Tunnel Vision That Costs Everything

Fixation is when you lock onto a goal like a laser, ignoring everything else. It's like driving through a storm with your eyes glued to the GPS, missing the road signs telling you to pull over. NASA's *Columbia* disaster is a heartbreaking example. In 2003, the Columbia Accident Investigation Board found that NASA's "keep-it-flying" culture was obsessed with a February 19 deadline to deliver a space station module. That date was "etched in stone," and leaders felt "under the gun." Engineers warned about foam debris damaging the shuttle's wing, but the fixation on the schedule drowned them out. The result? A tragedy that cost seven lives and shook NASA to its core.

I've been there, too. Early in my career, I was tasked with leading an underperforming shop in the 90th FS and turn it around before a major Higher Headquarters (HQ) inspection. Under a tight deadline, I pushed my team to deliver, brushing off concerns about overworked staff. We hit the deadline, but morale tanked, and my entire team wanted to quit and be moved to other units. My fixation on the goal cost me more than I gained…the trust and support of my team. It took me years and a ton of personal growth/development to regain their trust. Great leaders don't just chase targets; they see the bigger picture—people, safety, values. Fixation blinds you, but perspective sets you free.

Rationalization: Justifying the Wrong Path

Rationalization is the voice in your head that says, "It's okay to bend the rules, just this once." It's how good people convince themselves that unethical choices are fine if the goal is big enough. Picture a beer company CEO, like the one we talked about in Chapter 1. His company's core value is responsible drinking, but he approves a sales commission plan to boost profits. Salespeople, chasing bonuses, start pushing beer to minors or overserving customers. When the headlines hit, the CEO's shocked—but he shouldn't be. He rationalized that the plan was "just business," ignoring the ethical red flags.

Rationalization is sneaky. It's the "end justifies the means" mindset that lets you sleep at night while you're cutting corners. I remember a time when I justified skipping a safety check to meet a deadline, telling myself, "It's fine, we've done this before." We got lucky—no one got hurt—but I learned that rationalization is a trap. Leaders don't justify shortcuts; they build bridges to integrity. The moment you hear yourself saying, "It's not a big deal," stop and ask, "Am I rationalizing something I'll regret?"

Detachment: Leading with a Cold Heart

Detachment is when you disconnect from the people your decisions affect. It's like leading from behind a glass wall—you see your team, but you don't feel their struggles. Imagine a corporate executive cutting employee healthcare to boost profits. He doesn't know the single mom who now can't afford her kid's medicine or the veteran relying on that coverage. Detached from their reality, he sees numbers, not lives. That's how detachment destroys trust and character.

I saw this firsthand in that unit I was pushing so hard to turn around. So focused on the mission, cutting costs, fixing training and improving the quality of the products we maintain, without even the slightest consideration of talking to my team. As I mentioned, morale plummeted, and productivity followed yet I couldn't figure out why...so I pushed harder. I wasn't a bad guy—I was just detached, treating people like line items, a means to an end. Great leaders stay connected. They walk the floor, listen to their team, and feel the weight of their decisions. Detachment makes it easy to ignore ethics; engagement makes it impossible.

Why These Symptoms Matter

Fixation, rationalization, and detachment aren't just personal flaws—they're leadership failures that ripple outward. Fixation costs lives, like in NASA's case. Rationalization erodes trust, as the beer company learned. Detachment breaks teams, as I personally experienced. These symptoms don't just hurt you; they hurt everyone who depends on your leadership. But here's the good news: You can spot them, stop them, and lead better.

Think about your own workplace. Have you ever been so focused on a goal that you missed a warning sign? Or justified a decision because "it's what the boss wants"? Maybe you've felt disconnected from your team, making choices that seemed fine on paper but hurt real people. These are signs of teleopathy, and recognizing them is the first step to breaking free.

Real-World Lessons: The NASA Tragedy

Let's go back to NASA's *Columbia* disaster to see these symptoms in action. The Columbia Accident Investigation Board didn't just blame foam debris—they pointed to NASA's culture. Leaders were fixated on a launch schedule, ignoring engineers' concerns about safety. They rationalized that past foam incidents hadn't caused crashes, so this one wouldn't either. And they were detached, failing to connect with the engineers who knew the risks or the astronauts who paid the price. In his writings, Professor Goodpaster called this an "uncanny reminder" of the 1986 *Challenger* disaster, where similar symptoms led to another tragedy.

NASA's story isn't about bad intentions—it's about leaders losing their way. They wanted to succeed, to advance science, to meet deadlines. But teleopathy blinded them to the human cost. As leaders, we have to ask: Are we repeating NASA's mistakes? Are we so driven by goals that we're missing the warning signs?

The Leadership Solution

Here's where you take control. Spotting teleopathy's symptoms is like checking your car's dashboard for warning lights. Ignore them, and you crash. Pay attention, and you stay on course. Let's look at how to tackle each symptom with practical wisdom you can use today.

From Fixation to Perspective: Great leaders zoom out. Instead of obsessing over one goal, they see the whole map—people, values, long-term impact. If NASA had paused to listen to engineers, they might have saved *Columbia*. Try this: Before you chase a goal, ask, "What am I missing? Who's affected?" That question alone can save you from tunnel vision.

From Rationalization to Frankness: Leaders tell the truth, even when it's hard. If you're tempted to justify a shortcut, stop and be honest with yourself. The beer company CEO could have avoided disaster by asking, "Does this plan honor our values?" Practice frankness by admitting when a goal pushes you toward unethical choices, then course-correct.

From Detachment to Engagement: Stay connected to your people. Walk the floor, listen to their concerns, feel their challenges. When I was pushing that team at the 90th FS, I didn't know my team's struggles because I never asked. Great leaders build bridges, not walls. Make it a habit to check in with your team, not just on results but on how they're doing.

Your Leadership Edge

Beating teleopathy isn't just about avoiding failure—it's about building a legacy. When you spot fixation, rationalization, and detachment, you're not just saving your team from a crisis;

you're showing them what real leadership looks like. People follow leaders they trust, and trust comes from integrity. As John Maxwell says, "Leadership is influence—nothing more, nothing less." When you lead with a clear conscience, you influence others to do the same.

I'll never forget how terrible I felt when I realized what I was doing and how hard I had worked to turn things around, to become a better leader, and make things right for my team. My team was broken and when I finally saw the signs—low morale, customer complaints, poor productivity, bad quality—and I knew something had to change...that something was me. I held a team meeting, admitted my own role in pushing too hard, and reset the focus on more ethical and achievable goals. Productivity dipped temporarily, but trust soared, and the team bounced back stronger. Within a year, we were recognized by HQ as the program of the year. That's the power of spotting teleopathy and acting on it.

Moving Forward

This chapter is your wake-up call. Teleopathy's symptoms—fixation, rationalization, detachment— are everywhere, but they don't have to define your leadership. In the chapters ahead, we'll explore ethical frameworks to keep you grounded, stories of leaders who beat teleopathy, and tools to build an ethical workplace. For now, commit to this: Watch

THE PURPOSE-DRIVEN LEADER

for the warning signs, and lead with the courage to
do what's right, not just what's easy.

Pause and Reflect

- Which of teleopathy's symptoms—fixation, rationalization, or detachment—have you seen in your workplace? How did they affect morale or outcomes?

- How can you stay connected to your team's needs while pursuing big goals?

Leadership Action Steps

1. **Create a Symptom Checklist**: Write down fixation, rationalization, and detachment. Before major decisions, check if any apply and adjust your approach.

2. **Hold Team Huddles**: Schedule weekly meetings to discuss ethical challenges openly. Ask your team, "Are we pushing too hard? Are we staying true to our values?"

Chapter 3: Leading with Ethics: Care, Virtue, and Duty

Let me share with you this hypothetical sorry about Sarah, a pastor who took over a struggling community church. She had big dreams: grow the congregation, renovate the building, and make a difference in her town. But in her zeal to succeed, she made a mistake. She adopted a corporate mindset, focusing on fundraising and attendance numbers like a CEO chasing profits. She pushed her volunteers to work long hours, ignored their burnout, and even cut community outreach to save money. Within a year, her congregation dwindled, and her best volunteers walked away. Sarah wasn't a bad leader—she just picked the wrong ethical playbook. Her story shows what happens when you misapply ethics in leadership, letting teleopathy sneak in and derail your mission.

In my Air Force days, I saw leaders wrestle with similar choices. One commander I worked with was so focused on mission success that he forgot to care for his team's well-being. Another tried to instill discipline but neglected the human side of leadership. Both were good people, but they missed the mark because they didn't anchor their decisions in the right ethical framework. That's what this chapter is about: using three powerful ethical lenses—care, virtue, and duty—to lead with integrity and keep teleopathy at bay. These aren't just theories; they're tools to make you the kind of leader others trust and follow.

Why Ethics Matter in Leadership

Leadership isn't just about results; it's about how you get there. Teleopathy, as we've seen, blinds you to the "how" when you're obsessed with the "what." In Chapter 2, we talked about spotting teleopathy's symptoms—fixation, rationalization, detachment. Now, we're going to arm you with three ethical frameworks to fight back. Think of them as your leadership compass, guiding you through the pressure of goals and deadlines. Care ethics, virtue theory, and duty theory aren't stuffy academic ideas—they're practical ways to lead with heart, character, and principle. Let's dive in and see how they work.

Care Ethics: Leading Like Family

Care ethics is about putting people first, treating them like family. It says you have a responsibility to look out for those who depend on you—your team, your customers, your community. Imagine a hospital director named Maria. Her hospital's budget was tight, and the board pushed her to cut staff to save money. But Maria knew her nurses were overworked, and patients were struggling. Instead of slashing jobs, she fought for her team, investing in training and better patient care. Her hospital didn't just survive—it became a community cornerstone, known for compassion.

That's care ethics in action: leading with empathy, not just efficiency.

Care ethics is your shield against teleopathy's detachment. When you're tempted to see people as numbers, care ethics pulls you back. It asks, "How will this decision affect the people I serve?" In my Air Force days, I had a Commander who lived this principle. He'd walk the hangar, talk to every mechanic, and ask about their families. When budget cuts loomed, he fought to keep their benefits, knowing their well-being fueled our mission. His team didn't just work for him—they trusted him. That's the power of leading like you care.

But here's the catch: Care ethics can go wrong if you misapply it. Imagine a church using care ethics to focus on long-term profits instead of spiritual growth. They might pamper their biggest donors, ignoring the needs of the broader congregation. That's teleopathy creeping in, twisting a good principle into a goal-obsessed trap. Great leaders use care ethics to build trust, not to chase the wrong goals.

Virtue Theory: Building a Character That Inspires

Virtue theory is about becoming a leader others admire—not for your results, but for your character (who you are). It's about building habits that balance your ambitions with integrity, like honesty, courage, and humility. Think of a nonprofit leader, we will call him James, who ran a youth mentoring program. His team was under pressure to secure grants, and he could've fudged numbers to impress funders. Instead, he chose transparency, even when it meant losing a grant. His honesty inspired his team to work harder, and they found new donors who valued their integrity. James didn't just lead a program—he built a legacy of virtue.

Virtue theory fights teleopathy's rationalization. When you're tempted to justify a shortcut, virtue theory reminds you to stick to your principles. I saw this in action with a colleague who refused to follow orders when he knew the orders were unlawful and could result in someone getting hurt or killed. His team (I was one of them) respected him for it, and their work stood the test of time. Virtue theory is like a muscle—you strengthen it by practicing good habits, like telling the truth or owning your mistakes…yes, all of them.

But misapply it, and you're in trouble. Imagine if an auto repair shop adopted virtue theory but focused on spiritual balance instead of practical service. They might spend all their time mentoring employees on personal growth, neglecting customers' cars. That's teleopathy again, fixating on the wrong goal and losing sight of the business's purpose. Virtue theory works when you align it with your mission, building a character that others can count on.

Duty Theory: Doing What's Right Because It's Right

Duty theory is simple but powerful: You know the difference between right and wrong, and it's your job to do what's right. It's the foundation of the golden rule—treat other people as you'd want to be treated as well as the platinum rule—treat other people as they want to be treated. Picture an auto repair shop owner, we will call him Tom, who lives by this principle. When a customer comes in with a tight budget, Tom could overcharge for unnecessary repairs. Instead, he fixes only what's needed, explains every cost, and even offers a discount to a struggling family. His customers keep coming back, and his shop thrives. That's duty theory: doing the right thing, no matter the pressure and yes...sometimes, no matter the cost.

Duty theory counters teleopathy's fixation. When you're obsessed with a goal, duty theory pulls you back to your moral compass. In my first Air Force assignment, I worked for a Staff Sergeant (SSgt) who refused to rush production and release equipment that didn't meet safety standards, even when it meant delaying a mission. His commitment to duty saved us from a potential disaster and served as a lesson I would carry with me for the rest of my career. Duty theory isn't about feelings—it's about principle, doing what's right because it's your responsibility.

But here's where it can go wrong: Imagine a hospital adopting duty theory but focusing only on following rules, not caring for patients' emotional needs. They might check every box but leave patients feeling like numbers. Teleopathy sneaks in when you fixate on rigid duties at the expense of human connection. Duty theory shines when you find harmony with care and virtue, ensuring you do right by everyone or at least try.

When Ethics Go Wrong: A Cautionary Tale

Let's tie this together with a hypothetical story. Meet Alex, CEO of a mid-sized retail chain. He wanted to make his company a beacon of ethics, so he adopted care ethics, focusing on employee well-being. He offered generous benefits and flexible hours, but he got fixated on keeping employees happy at all costs. To fund those benefits, he raised prices, ignoring customers who couldn't afford them. Sales dropped, and the company struggled. Then, Alex tried virtue theory, emphasizing honesty and transparency. But he overcorrected, spending more time on team-building retreats than on business strategy, and profits tanked further. Finally, he turned to duty theory, enforcing strict rules to cut costs, but he became detached, alienating his team. In each case, Alex's good intentions were derailed by teleopathy—fixation, rationalization, or detachment—because he misapplied the ethical frameworks. Think this couldn't happen, you're wrong. I've seen it happen myself. A former supervisor of mine, a good man doing what he believed was right, lost his way and in the end lost his career because he didn't understand this framework and how to properly apply it.

Alex's story shows that ethical frameworks are powerful, but only if you use them wisely. Care ethics needs balance to avoid neglecting other stakeholders. Virtue theory requires focus to stay relevant to your mission. Duty theory demands flexibility to keep human connection alive. Teleopathy can twist even the best intentions, but great leaders know how to apply these frameworks to stay on track.

Your Leadership Compass

These three frameworks—care, virtue, and duty— are your tools to fight teleopathy. They're not just theories; they're ways to live out your leadership. Care ethics keeps you connected to your people, fighting detachment. Virtue theory builds your character, stopping rationalization. Duty theory anchors you to what's right, breaking fixation. Together, they form a compass that guides you through the toughest decisions.

Think about your own leadership. Which of these frameworks resonates with you? Maybe you're a natural at caring for your team, like Maria the hospital director. Or you're driven by duty, like Tom the shop owner. Whatever your style, these frameworks give you a way to check yourself against teleopathy's pull. As John Maxwell says, "Leadership is influence—nothing more, nothing less." When you lead with care, virtue, and duty, you influence others to do the same, building a workplace where ethics thrive.

Real-World Inspiration

Let's look at a company that gets it right. Costco, the retail giant, lives out a blend of these frameworks. They care for employees with high wages and benefits, fostering loyalty. They build a culture of virtue, emphasizing fairness and transparency with customers. And they operate with a sense of duty, treating suppliers and communities with respect. Costco's leaders aren't perfect, but they show how ethical frameworks can combat teleopathy, balancing profit with principle. Their success—steady growth and a loyal customer base—proves that leading with ethics isn't just right; it's smart.

Making It Practical

How do you put these frameworks into action? Start small, but start now. If you lean toward care ethics, spend 10 minutes a day listening to your team's concerns. If virtue theory is your thing, commit to one honest action daily, like admitting a mistake. If duty theory drives you, write down your "golden rule" and check every decision against it. These small steps build habits that keep teleopathy at bay.

THE PURPOSE-DRIVEN LEADER

I'll never forget a leader I worked with who mastered this balance. She ran a supply chain team under intense pressure to cut costs. Instead of slashing jobs, she used care ethics to protect her team, virtue theory to stay transparent with stakeholders, and duty theory to ensure every decision was fair. Her team didn't just meet goals— they exceeded them, with trust and morale intact. That's the kind of leader you can be.

Moving Forward

Care, virtue, and duty are your weapons against teleopathy's pull. In the chapters ahead, we'll explore how to apply these frameworks in global contexts, use technology to teach ethics, and build a culture where integrity wins. For now, pick one framework and start using it today. Your team is watching, and your leadership can change the game.

Pause and Reflect

- Which ethical framework—care, virtue, or duty—resonates most with your leadership style? Why?

- How might misapplying one of these frameworks lead to unintended consequences in your workplace?

THE PURPOSE-DRIVEN LEADER

Leadership Action Steps

1. **Choose Your Framework**: Pick one ethical framework (care, virtue, or duty) and write down how you can apply it to a current challenge. Share it with your team.

2. **Create a Team Mantra**: Develop a short phrase based on care, virtue, or duty (e.g., "We care for each other," "We lead with honesty," "We do what's right"). Use it to guide team decisions.

Chapter 4: Ethics Across Borders: Navigating Global Challenges

Let me take you back to the 1990s, when Nike was the king of athletic wear. Their sneakers were everywhere, from basketball courts to city streets. But behind the swoosh logo, a storm was brewing. Reports surfaced that Nike's factories in Southeast Asia were using child labor and paying workers pennies for long hours in harsh conditions. Nike's leaders weren't evil—they saw a chance to cut costs and compete globally. But their obsession with low prices blinded them to the human cost. When the headlines hit, customers boycotted, and Nike's reputation took a beating. The lesson? Leading in a global world means balancing profit with ethics, or you risk losing everything. That's what this chapter is about: navigating the ethical minefield of global business without falling into teleopathy's trap.

In my Air Force days, I worked on international missions where cultural differences could make or break a project. I remember a time when I was in the Middle East and we were working with a foreign military unit. Our team was focused on mission efficiency and effectiveness, pushing for quick precise results, but our partners valued long lunches, giving them time to pray and meditate. Our rush to "get it done" nearly derailed the mission until we had to slow down and respect their ways or the entire mission would have failed. That experience taught me that global leadership isn't just about goals—it's about understanding people, their values and way of life. Teleopathy can turn good intentions into ethical disasters when you lead across borders, but with the right approach, you can build bridges instead of walls.

The Global Leadership Challenge

The world is smaller than ever. Your supply chain might stretch from Shanghai to São Paulo, your team could span five continents, and your customers could be anywhere. But with that global reach comes a big challenge: How do you lead ethically when cultures, values, and laws differ? Teleopathy makes this harder. It's the voice that says, "Just keep costs low," or "Do what works here," ignoring the ethical fallout. In Chapter 3, we explored care, virtue, and duty as your ethical compass. Now, we'll apply them to the global stage, where teleopathy can twist good intentions into cultural missteps or moral failures.

Take Nike's story I introduce at the beginning of this chapter. When they moved manufacturing to countries like Indonesia and Vietnam to cut costs. Their goal was simple: stay competitive in a cutthroat market. But they didn't account for local labor practices, like child labor or low wages, that clashed with Western expectations. When activists exposed these practices, Nike faced protests and lost customer trust. Their fixation on profits—a classic teleopathy symptom—blinded them to the ethical and cultural implications. Great leaders don't just chase global success; they navigate the world with eyes wide open.

The Trap of Moral Institutionalism

Let's talk about a big idea: moral institutionalism. Scholars like Wim Dubbink and Ben van de Ven describe it as the push to impose universal ethical standards, often Western ones, on every culture. It sounds noble—bring order, end suffering, uphold justice. But it can backfire. Imagine a U.S. company setting up a factory in a small Asian country where kids work by age 11 to support their families. The company bans child labor to align with Western values, but this leaves local families struggling, unable to afford food. The company meant well, but their fixation on one ethical standard ignored the local culture, causing harm instead of good. That's teleopathy at work, turning a good intention into an ethical misstep.

I saw this for myself in 1991 while serving with the US Air Force Air Demonstration Team, the Thunderbirds. We were in the middle of our European Tour and had stopped in Germany for three days to repair aircraft and pick up some needed parts. While there, our Commander was pushing hard for the local government to allow him and the other pilots fly some practice shows so they could stay at the peak of proficiency, and he couldn't understand why he was getting so much resistance. He believed he and his pilots had every right to practice based on the agreements we had with the host country and tension was building on both sides. Then he discovered that in 1988 at the same air base we were at, there was an accident and 70 people (3 pilots, 67 spectators) lost their lives. After learning this he understood their resistance and abandoned the idea of doing any practice shows while we were there. Moral institutionalism can feel right and can even feel like the high road, but it risks imposing your values on others, alienating stakeholders and fueling resentment. Great leaders respect differences while holding firm to core principles.

A Pluralistic Approach: Robert Audi's Wisdom

So, how do you lead ethically across borders? Robert Audi, a professor at Notre Dame, offers a solution: pluralistic ethics. This means operating under your ethical norms while respecting the values of the cultures you work with. It's like conducting an orchestra—every culture plays a different note, but the harmony is integrity. Imagine a tech company opening a factory in India. They pay fair wages by local standards, respect cultural traditions like family work roles, but maintain strict safety standards to protect workers. They're not forcing Western rules or abandoning their values— they're finding a balance that works for everyone.

Audi's approach fights teleopathy's rationalization. Instead of saying, "It's okay to bend our ethics to fit local norms," you find a way to uphold integrity while honoring differences. Think of it this way, Joe once worked with a logistics team partnering with a Middle Eastern supplier. His company valued transparency, but the supplier relied on personal relationships over contracts. Instead of pushing Joe's companies way, they built trust through face-to-face meetings, keeping their ethical standards while respecting the supplier's culture. The result? A stronger partnership and better outcomes. Pluralistic ethics isn't easy, but it's how you lead globally without losing your soul.

When Good Intentions Go Wrong

Let's look at another hypothetical story to drive this home. Meet Priya, a CEO of a clothing brand expanding into Bangladesh. She wanted to help a struggling community, so she built a factory, offering jobs to locals. But her team, fixated on keeping costs low, ignored local labor laws allowing longer work hours. They rationalized it, saying, "We're giving them jobs they wouldn't have otherwise." When reports of worker exhaustion hit the news, customers accused Priya's company of exploitation. Her good intentions—helping a community—were derailed by teleopathy, as her team detached from the workers' reality and fixated on profit margins.

Priya's story shows that global leadership is a tightrope. You can't just export your ethics or adopt local practices blindly. Teleopathy sneaks in when you focus on one goal—like cost-cutting or "helping"—without considering the cultural and ethical fallout. Great leaders walk that tightrope with care, balancing their values with the needs of the people they serve.

Real-World Inspiration: Levi Strauss & Co.

Contrast Priya's story with Levi Strauss & Co. In the 1990s, they faced similar challenges as Nike but took a different path. When reports surfaced about poor conditions in their overseas factories, Levi's leaders didn't rationalize or detach. They created a global code of conduct, setting standards for fair wages and safe conditions while working with local partners to respect cultural norms. They engaged with communities, listened to workers, and invested in improvements. The result? Levi's rebuilt trust, strengthened their brand, and showed that ethical leadership can win globally. They didn't let teleopathy blind them—they led with perspective, frankness, and engagement.

Your Global Leadership Playbook

Leading across borders isn't for the faint of heart, but it's where great leaders shine. Here's how to navigate global challenges without falling into teleopathy's trap, Maxwell-style:

See the Whole Picture: Don't fixate on one goal, like profits or compliance. Ask, "How does this decision affect every stakeholder— local workers, global customers, my team?" Perspective keeps you grounded.

Be Honest, Not Convenient: Rationalization loves to whisper, "It's how things are done here." Fight it with frankness. If a practice feels wrong, speak up and find a way to do right by everyone.

Stay Connected: Detachment is easy when you're thousands of miles from your supply chain. Engage with local partners—visit their communities, listen to their stories, feel their challenges. Connection builds trust.

Can you imagine this: A leader of a global nonprofit working in rural Africa, where local customs clash with her organization's values. Instead of imposing rules, she spends weeks learning from community leaders, finding ways to align her mission with their needs. As a result, her project thrives because she led with respect and integrity. That's the kind of leaders we want to see, and you can be.

Making It Practical

You don't need to run a global company to apply these lessons. Whether you're managing a diverse team or working with international clients, you can lead ethically across borders. Start by learning one cultural norm from a colleague or partner this week. Ask questions, listen deeply, and check if your decisions respect their values while upholding your own. Small steps like these build habits that keep teleopathy at bay.

Moving Forward

Global leadership is your chance to make a difference, not just a profit. In the chapters ahead, we'll explore how technology can spread ethical values, how leaders set the tone for integrity, and how to build a workplace where ethics win. For now, commit to this: Lead with respect for every culture, but never compromise your conscience. Your influence can change the world, one ethical decision at a time.

Pause and Reflect

- How do you handle ethical dilemmas when working with different cultures?

- What's one way you can respect cultural values without compromising your principles?

Leadership Action Steps

1. **Learn Local Norms**: Partner with a local leader or colleague to understand one cultural practice in your workplace or supply chain. Use it to inform your next decision.

2. **Create a Global Ethics Policy**: Draft a short policy that balances your organization's values with flexibility for cultural differences. Share it with your team for feedback.

Chapter 5: Technology as a Leadership Tool for Ethics

Imagine you're a manager at a global firm, juggling deadlines and a team spread across three continents. You're under pressure to hit sales targets, and teleopathy's whispering in your ear: "Just focus on the numbers." But then you stumble across a blog post that stops you cold. It's a story about a company that lost everything by cutting ethical corners, and it hits home. You share it with your team, sparking a conversation about values that changes how you lead. That's the power of technology—it's not just a tool for efficiency; it's a megaphone for ethics, amplifying your voice as a leader to fight teleopathy's grip.

In my Air Force days, I saw technology transform how we communicated. We used digital briefings to align global teams on mission priorities, but I noticed something else: When we shared stories of integrity—like when Airman speak up about safety issues or the quality assurance office retraining a team member to prevent future mistakes—it inspired everyone. Technology didn't just deliver data; it spread values. That's what this chapter is about: using blogs, podcasts, videos, and more to teach ethics, keep teleopathy at bay, and build a workplace where integrity wins. In a world where goals can blind us, technology is your leadership edge to keep ethics front and center.

The Power of Technology in Leadership

We live in a digital age. Your smartphone connects you to the world, your inbox buzzes with updates, and your team collaborates on platforms like Zoom or Slack. But technology isn't just for getting work done—it's for shaping how work is done. Teleopathy thrives when leaders fixate on goals, rationalize shortcuts, or detach from their teams, as we saw in Chapters 2 and 3. Technology can fight back by spreading ethical ideas, sparking conversations, and keeping values alive. Whether it's a blog post, a podcast, or a viral video, these tools let you reach your team—no matter where they are—and inspire them to lead with integrity.

Think about it: A single post can change a company's culture. A podcast can teach thousands about ethics. A video can make complex ideas simple and compelling. These aren't just tech tricks; they're leadership tools to combat teleopathy's pull. Let's explore how real leaders are using them to make a difference, and how you can, too.

Real-World Examples: Technology in Action

Let's start with a story from the blogosphere. In 2012, James Hoban wrote a blog post called "What Are Values, Morals, and Ethics?" that went viral among business leaders. He said, "Great moral values, like truth, freedom, and charity, protect and enhance life when they work right." Simple, but powerful. That post reached executives from New

York to Nairobi, shaping how they viewed ethics. Imagine a manager in South America reading it and rethinking how they treat suppliers. That's technology breaking through teleopathy's fixation, reminding leaders to prioritize values over profits.

Then there's Trevor Bromell, who produced a podcast series for the Institute of Chartered Accountants in England and Wales. His "Acting With Integrity" series laid out clear expectations for ethical behavior, reaching employees worldwide. One episode shared a story of an accountant who caught a billing error and fixed it, even though it meant missing a deadline. That story stuck with listeners, fighting rationalization by showing that integrity trumps short-term wins. Bromell's podcast didn't just inform—it inspired, proving that technology can make ethics personal and real.

In 2009, a group of students—Laura Busam, Brittany Dickson, Andy Doster, and Kenny Rod— created a YouTube video called "Business Ethics Through Film: Monsters Inc." They used the Pixar movie to show how easy it is to make bad ethical choices, even with good intentions. In the film, a monster company was scaring human kids to power their city, unfortunately many kids were becoming desensitized to being scared and the company was struggling. The company CEO, Mr. Henry J. Waternoose, felt immense pressure from the board to increase production, so he orchestrated the abduction of a little human girl in order to test an experimental scream extractor, rationalizing it as "necessary to save his company." The video went viral, teaching business students and leaders alike to spot teleopathy's symptoms. It's proof that a fun, engaging story can make ethics stick in a way memos never will.

A Case Study: Technology Transforming a Company

Let's tie this together with a real-world example. Meet Katie Lawler, EVP and Global Chief Ethics Officer at US Bank. Her company was growing fast, but ethical challenges were creeping in amid pandemic pressures and operational stress—teams pushing aggressive targets and rationalizing shortcuts to meet goals. Katie knew she had to act, so she turned to technology to humanize ethics and build trust. She launched the "Captain's Log" blog series on Microsoft Viva Engage, sharing daily relatable stories of personal mishaps, burnout, and family life to connect with employees during isolation.

Next, Katie created the "Ethics RideShare" video series, featuring casual car conversations with executives (filmed on GoPro cameras) discussing values and ethical dilemmas, like embedding consumer bank principles in daily work. The videos were deployed on the internal platform USBTV and the intranet homepage. Finally, she produced the "Ethics Mythbusters" short video series—quick 90-120 second iPad recordings debunking misconceptions, such as the ethics line being

68

ineffective or restrictions on second jobs, edited with simple animations and shared via Viva Engage.

Within a year, these initiatives transformed engagement: thousands of blog followers, high video views competing with CEO content, viral posts reducing feelings of isolation, and increased employee feedback and trust. Katie didn't just use technology—she wielded it like a leadership tool to beat teleopathy, fostering a culture where ethics trumped short-term pressures.

The Future: Technology's Next Frontier

Technology isn't standing still, and neither should your leadership. Imagine virtual reality training where your team faces ethical dilemmas in a simulated boardroom, practicing how to resist teleopathy's pull. Or AI-driven dashboards that flag decisions at risk of fixation, like a sales target that ignores customer needs. These tools are coming, and they'll make ethical leadership easier and more engaging. But you don't need to wait for the future. Blogs, podcasts, and videos are here now, and they're powerful enough to change your workplace today.

In my Air Force days, when I worked at the Pentagon, I used technology to host monthly virtual Chief's Panels, where anyone from any level could call in and ask questions or share information. At first, some people resisted because they feared what would come from it but over time, people grew to see it as the positive force for change it was intended to be. As leaders, we are often sheltered from the truth, filters between us and the lowest levels remove vital pieces of the puzzle which are critical to solve issues. I would tell my people all the time "we can't fix what we don't know is broken." and by focusing on solving the problem and not looking to place blame, over time we earned their trust. Doing this, technology amplified our values, and it can do the same for you. Whether you're leading a small team or a global firm, you can use digital tools to spread ethics, fight teleopathy, and inspire your people.

The Leadership Opportunity

Here's where you come in. Technology isn't just for IT—it's for every leader who wants to make a difference. It's your megaphone to share values, your classroom to teach integrity, and your bridge to connect with your team. Teleopathy loves silence, thriving when ethical conversations are rare. But when you use technology to spark those conversations, you break teleopathy's grip. As you read in a previous chapter, John Maxwell says, "Leadership is influence—nothing more, nothing less." When you use blogs, podcasts, or videos to champion ethics, you influence your team to do the same.

Think about your workplace. Could a blog post inspire your team to speak up about unethical practices? Could a podcast share stories of integrity that stick with your people? Technology makes it easy to reach everyone, from the front line to the C-suite. And it's not just about reaching them—it's about engaging them, making ethics real and relatable.

Making It Practical

You don't need to be a tech guru to use these tools. Start small, but start now. Write a short blog post for your team about a time you faced an ethical dilemma and how you handled it. Record a five-minute podcast sharing a story of integrity from your workplace. Or create a quick video using your phone, explaining one ethical principle from Chapter 3—care, virtue, or duty—and how it applies to your team. These small steps can start big conversations, building a culture where ethics beat teleopathy every time.

As a Senior Noncommissioned Officer (SNCO) at Travis AFB in California, I used technology to express my values and promote leadership development in a weekly email I called Food For Thought. As an organization, we were in the process of rebuilding the shop after it had failed a major HHQ inspection and because many of our people deployed to the Middle East, I feared when they returned, they would not have made the cultural shift the rest of the team at home was going through. By sending these weekly emails, when members returned they were able to seamlessly integrate into the new way of doing things and we were able to turn the organization around much more quickly. That's the power of technology in leadership.

The Limits of Technology

A quick word of caution: Technology is a tool, not a cure-all. It can spread ethical ideas, but it can't replace your example. If you share a podcast about integrity but rationalize shortcuts in your own work, your team will notice. Teleopathy thrives on inconsistency, so make sure your actions match your message. Use technology to amplify your leadership, not to hide behind it.

Moving Forward

Technology is your ally in the fight against teleopathy. It's how you share stories, teach values, and connect with your team, no matter where they are. In the chapters ahead, we'll explore how leaders set the ethical tone, build cultures of integrity, and learn from failure. For now, commit to this: Use one digital tool this week to spark an ethical conversation. Your influence can change your workplace, one post, podcast, or video at a time.

Pause and Reflect

- How can you use technology to inspire ethical behavior in your team?

- What's one digital tool you could leverage to share your values?

Leadership Action Steps

1. **Launch a Team Blog or Podcast**: Share a short post or recording about an ethical challenge you faced and how you resolved it. Invite your team to contribute their own stories.

2. **Use Interactive Modules**: Create a simple online quiz or scenario-based training to help your team practice spotting teleopathy's symptoms. Share it via email or your company's platform.

Chapter 6: The Leader's Role: Setting the Ethical Tone

Let me tell you about a company that seemed unstoppable. Volkswagen, the German automaker, was a global giant in 2015, known for its "clean diesel" cars. But behind the scenes, leaders were chasing a dangerous goal: dominate the U.S. market at any cost. To meet strict emissions standards, they installed software to cheat tests, making their cars appear eco-friendly while polluting the air. When the truth came out, Volkswagen paid billions in fines, lost customer trust, and saw its reputation crumble. The culprit? Teleopathy. Leaders were so fixated on market share, rationalizing deception, and detached from the consequences that they betrayed their own values. This chapter is about one truth: As a leader, you set the ethical tone, and if you don't, teleopathy will.

In my Air Force days, I saw how a leader's actions shaped everything. One commander I worked with was under pressure to boost mission readiness. Instead of cutting corners, he held daily huddles, listened to his team, and made it clear that safety came first. His integrity inspired us to follow suit, and our unit thrived. That's the power of a leader who sets the right tone. In Chapter 2, we identified teleopathy's symptoms—fixation, rationalization, detachment—and in Chapter 3, we explored ethical frameworks to fight them. Now, we'll focus on you, the leader, and how your choices can build a workplace where ethics win.

The Leader's Influence

Remember "Leadership is influence—nothing more, nothing less." Your team watches you—how you make decisions, handle pressure, and treat people. If you chase goals at the expense of values, they'll do the same. If you model integrity, they'll follow. Teleopathy thrives when leaders send mixed signals, like Volkswagen's executives who preached innovation but practiced deception. But when you set an ethical tone, you create a culture where teleopathy can't take root.

Think about your workplace. Your team looks to you for cues. If you ignore ethical red flags to hit a target, you're telling them it's okay to do the same. But if you pause, ask tough questions, and prioritize what's right, you're building a team that trusts you and each other. Your influence is your superpower—use it to fight teleopathy, not fuel it.

Volkswagen: A Cautionary Tale

Let's dive into the Volkswagen emissions scandal a bit more, a textbook case of teleopathy in leadership. VW's goal was clear: become the world's top carmaker by conquering the U.S. market. But U.S. emissions standards were tough, and VW's diesel engines couldn't meet them without sacrificing performance. Instead of innovating, leaders approved "defeat devices"—software that faked clean emissions during tests. They were fixated on market dominance, rationalized cheating as "necessary," and detached from the environmental and human impact. When the scandal broke, VW faced $18 billion in fines, recalled millions of cars, and lost consumer trust. CEO Martin Winterkorn resigned, and the company's stock plummeted.

Volkswagen's leaders weren't monsters—they were talented people who lost their way. Their obsession with goals blinded them to ethics, proving that even the biggest companies can fall when leaders fail to set the right tone. Imagine if VW's leaders had paused to ask, "Is this right?" or listened to engineers who raised concerns. They could've avoided disaster and built a legacy of integrity instead.

Goodpaster's Playbook: Perspective, Frankness, Engagement

To set an ethical tone, you need a playbook, and Professor Goodpaster gives us a great one: perspective, frankness, and engagement. These aren't just ideas—they're leadership habits that keep teleopathy at bay. Let's break them down with stories that show how they work.

Perspective: See the Big Picture

Perspective is about zooming out to see the whole map—people, values, long-term impact—not just the goal in front of you. In Chapter 2, we saw how NASA's fixation on a launch schedule led to the *Columbia* disaster. A leader with perspective would've listened to engineers' warnings and prioritized safety. I once worked with a commander who faced a similar choice. Under pressure to deploy a new system, he heard concerns about glitches. Instead of pushing forward, he delayed the rollout, saving us from a costly failure. Perspective saved the day.

As a leader, perspective means asking, "What's the cost of this goal? Who's affected?" It's like checking your blind spots before changing lanes. Without it, you're driving toward trouble.

Frankness: Tell the Truth, Always

Frankness is about being honest, even when it's tough. Volkswagen's leaders rationalized their deception, telling themselves it was "just business." A frank leader would've admitted, "This is wrong," and found another way. I saw frankness in action with a logistics officer who refused to sign off on a rushed shipment. It delayed a project, but his honesty built trust with the team. When you're tempted to justify a shortcut, stop and speak the truth—to yourself and your team.

Frankness fights teleopathy's rationalization. It's not always easy, but it's always right. As Maxwell says, "People don't care how much you know until they know how much you care." Show you care by being honest, even when it stings.

Engagement: Stay Connected

Engagement means staying close to your team, feeling their challenges, and listening to their voices. Volkswagen's leaders were detached, ignoring engineers who knew the truth. Contrast that with a leader I worked with who ran a maintenance crew. Under pressure to cut costs, she walked the hangar daily, talking to mechanics about their concerns. When budget cuts loomed, she fought for her team, keeping morale high. Her engagement built a team that trusted her, even in tough times.

Engagement fights detachment, keeping you grounded in your team's reality. It's not just about meetings—it's about connecting heart-to-heart, showing your team they matter.

A Real-World Turnaround

Let's look at a leader who got it right. In 2008, Howard Schultz returned as CEO of Starbucks after stepping away in 2000. The company had been chasing aggressive growth targets—thousands of new stores, new products, and rapid expansion. In the process, the brand lost its soul: coffee quality slipped, stores felt generic, baristas were overstretched, and customers were leaving. Teleopathy had taken hold—fixation on expansion goals led to rationalization of shortcuts and detachment from core values and stakeholders.

Schultz refused to look the other way. He acted decisively to break the trap:

- He closed all 7,100 U.S. stores for three hours to retrain baristas on espresso-making fundamentals, signaling that quality and customer experience mattered more than speed.
- He held town halls and listening sessions with employees to hear their struggles and frustrations directly (engagement).
- He set clear ethical and cultural guidelines, publicly admitting the company had drifted from its roots and recommitting to the "third place" experience (frankness).
- He aligned goals with stakeholder needs—refocusing on customers (better coffee and atmosphere), employees (training and respect), and communities (ethical sourcing) rather than unchecked expansion (perspective).

Within a year, customer traffic and sales rebounded. The stock price recovered dramatically, employee morale improved, and Starbucks rebuilt its reputation as a values-driven company. Schultz didn't just meet targets—he reset the ethical tone that changed the entire organization.

This is what breaking teleopathy looks like: recognizing when goals have gone off course, engaging stakeholders honestly, and realigning with purpose. It's not easy, but it works.

Your Leadership Moment

You're the one who sets the tone. Your team doesn't need a perfect leader—just one who's real, honest, and connected. Teleopathy thrives when leaders chase goals blindly, but you can stop it by modeling perspective, frankness, and engagement. Think about your workplace. Are you sending the right signals? If you're fixated on a goal, rationalizing a shortcut, or detached from your team, it's time to reset.

I'll never forget the moment I discovered this for myself. During my time at the Pentagon as the Aircrew Flight Equipment career field, one of my jobs was to ensure we were making the best use of the taxpayers' dollars. Shortly after taking my position, I became aware of a number of positions we had which were coded as "jump" positions, meaning people were being paid monthly to jump out of perfectly good airplanes using parachutes.

Because I didn't see a need for the number of jump positions we had and the military was under immense pressure from the Obama Administration to cut costs, I sent out a notice to all the Major Command Functional Managers, requesting them to justify their jump positions or risk losing them. For those not familiar with the military, this would be the equivalent of a Senior Corporate Executive sending a notice to all their regional managers.

Once the deadline had come and passed, there were several positions we had identified as not having adequate justification to support. Of course, doing what we believed was right, we started the work of removing the jump code from those positions. As we were working through this, we received a call from the Air Force Academy. It would seem they were having trouble finding Aircrew Flight Equipment personnel with the right qualifications to fill their positions. As it turned out, for the person to meet their requirements for being an instructor, they had to have performed a large number of parachute jumps. The only way for them to get these jumps was by being assigned to one of the jump coded positions we had in the field, positions like the ones we had just started to remove.

Now we were in a bit of a pickle (ok, I was in a pickle). We needed to make the best use of the taxpayers' money but we also need to make sure we were not allowing the mission at the Air Force Academy to suffer from our doing it. This was the perfect time for a second look at the program and the creation of a new action plan for how we were going to move forward. After reviewing the justification previously submitted by the Major Command Functional Managers, it was clear the positions we had removed were still needed but were not in the right places. We also noticed that the numbers in some of the Special Forces and Tactical units were not as high as they needed to be. When it was all said and done, we ended up increasing the number of jump positions throughout the career field. This allowed us to meet the desires of the Major Commands and ensure the right number of folks were in the process of growing to meet the future demands of the Air Force Academy. By doing what was needed and right, we gained the clarity in our purpose to successfully push back against the pressure to cut the budget and ensure the future success of our mission.

Consider for a moment how different this would have played out had I allowed Teleopathy to take over. If I hadn't been receptive to the idea my original decision could have been wrong or if I had stubbornly stuck to my position rather than admit I may have made a mistake. Chances are very good no one would have known for a few years, until after I retired. However, when they found out, it would have been too late to correct the issue. The mission at the Air Force Academy would have suffered until they could get the required jump positions back on the books and the people qualified to fill them. This example taught me that leadership isn't about being the loudest or always being correct—it's about being the clearest voice for what's right. It's not about being right, it's about getting it right.

Making It Practical

Setting an ethical tone starts with small steps. This week, try one of these: Hold a team huddle and ask, "Are we staying true to our values?" Be honest about a mistake you made and how you fixed it. Or spend 10 minutes listening to a team member's concerns without an agenda. These actions show your team that ethics matter, and they'll follow your lead.

Moving Forward

Your role as a leader is to light the way, not add to the darkness. By setting an ethical tone, you fight teleopathy and build a workplace where integrity wins. In the chapters ahead, we'll explore how to create a culture of ethics, learn from failure, and build frameworks for tough decisions. For now, commit to this: Be the leader your team looks to for what's right, not just what's easy.

Pause and Reflect

- What's one way your leadership style influences your team's ethics?

- How can you show your team that integrity matters more than results?

Leadership Action Steps

1. **Create a Leadership Pledge**: Write a one-sentence commitment to lead with integrity (e.g., "I will prioritize ethics in every decision"). Share it with your team.

2. **Hold Ethics Check-Ins**: Schedule quarterly meetings to discuss ethical challenges and reinforce your team's commitment to values.

Chapter 7: Building a Culture of Integrity

Let me take you to the rugged coast of California, where a company called Patagonia is doing something remarkable. While other outdoor brands chased profits, Patagonia built a culture around protecting the planet. They gave employees time to surf, donated profits to environmental causes, and made gear from recycled materials. Their founder, Yvon Chouinard, didn't just talk about values—he lived them, creating a workplace where integrity wasn't a slogan but a way of life. The result? Loyal employees, devoted customers, and a brand that thrives. Patagonia shows us that a culture of integrity doesn't just fight teleopathy—it wins.

In my Air Force days, I saw the power of culture firsthand. One unit I served in was struggling with low morale and ethical lapses. As I stepped in, set clear values—teamwork, honesty, respect—and made them real through daily actions. I praised people for flagging a safety issue, even if it delayed a mission. I held open forums where everyone could speak up. Within months, the unit transformed— people (not all of them but enough to make a positive difference) trusted each other, and performance soared. That's what this chapter is about: building a workplace culture where integrity beats teleopathy every time, so your team doesn't just survive but thrives.

Why Culture Matters

Your workplace culture is like the soil in a garden—what you plant in it grows. If you plant goals without values, teleopathy takes root, sprouting fixation, rationalization, and detachment, as we saw in Chapter 2. But if you plant integrity—through transparency, accountability, and engagement—you grow a team that trusts each other and does what's right. In Chapter 6, we talked about how leaders set the ethical tone. Now, we'll go deeper, showing you how to build a culture that makes ethics the heartbeat of your organization.

Think about your workplace. Is it a place where people feel safe to speak up about ethical concerns? Or do they keep quiet, fearing backlash? A culture of integrity isn't built by accident—it's crafted by leaders who make values non-negotiable. As John Maxwell says, "A leader is one who knows the way, goes the way, and shows the way." Your culture is how you show the way, and it's your best weapon against teleopathy.

Patagonia: A Model of Integrity

Let's dive into Patagonia's story. Founded by Yvon Chouinard, Patagonia didn't just sell outdoor gear—they lived their mission to "save our home planet." They embedded integrity into their culture in three ways: transparency, accountability, and engagement. They were transparent about their supply chain, admitting flaws and working to fix them. They held themselves accountable, donating 1% of sales to environmental causes since 1985. And they engaged employees, giving them flexibility to balance work and life, like closing offices for a day of activism. Patagonia's culture fought teleopathy by aligning every goal with their values.

Contrast that with Google's early days. Their motto, "Don't Be Evil," was a bold promise to prioritize ethics. But as the company grew, some leaders lost sight of it, chasing growth over integrity. In 2018, employees protested Google's work on a censored search engine for China, feeling it betrayed their values. Google's story shows that even a strong motto can falter if the culture doesn't back it up. Patagonia's success proves that a culture rooted in integrity can withstand teleopathy's pull, delivering results and respect.

The Pillars of an Ethical Culture

Building a culture of integrity isn't magic—it's method. Three pillars make it happen: transparency, accountability, and engagement. Let's break them down with stories and practical steps you can use today.

Transparency: Let the Truth Shine

Transparency means being open about your decisions, successes, and mistakes. It fights teleopathy's rationalization by making it hard to hide shortcuts. A powerful real-world example is Satya Nadella's return to Microsoft as CEO in 2014. The company had become fixated on crushing competitors and dominating markets, leading to a toxic "know-it-all" culture, internal rankings that encouraged cutthroat behavior, and rationalized shortcuts to hit aggressive targets. Nadella recognized the drift and chose radical transparency instead of denial.

He openly admitted the company had lost its way—publicly declaring a shift from "know-it-all" to "learn-it-all." He replaced forced stack-ranking with growth-mindset reviews, shared his own vulnerabilities (including personal stories about his family and growth), and encouraged employees to speak up about failures without fear. In memos and town halls, he admitted past missteps, like the "scroogled" campaign against Google, and invited honest feedback across the organization. This openness made it impossible to rationalize unethical or short-sighted tactics—truth became the default.

The result? Trust soared, innovation accelerated, employee morale improved dramatically, and Microsoft's market value grew from around $300 billion to over $3 trillion. Nadella didn't hide risks or failures; he let the truth shine, and it transformed the entire culture.

Transparency isn't just honesty; it's a culture where truth is the default, and teleopathy has nowhere to hide.

In my previous example about the jump positions, I nearly eliminated in the Air Force. My transparency about my mistake greatly enhanced my relationship with the other Chiefs in my career field. It showed I was willing to admit my mistakes, ask for help in making things right, and perhaps most importantly…demonstrated to them it was safe from them to do it as well. Nothing good grows in darkness, leaders need to be the light and transparency is the tool required to do it. Transparency didn't weaken my leadership—it strengthened it.

Accountability: Own Your Actions

Accountability means holding yourself and your team to high standards, no excuses. It fights teleopathy's fixation by tying every goal to values and purpose. A powerful real-world example is Paul Polman's time as CEO of Unilever starting in 2009. The company was under intense pressure from shareholders to deliver short-term profits and stock price growth, leading to a culture fixated on quarterly earnings targets. Teams rationalized cost-cutting and shortcuts that compromised long-term sustainability and brand integrity.

Polman refused to play along. He publicly announced Unilever would no longer provide quarterly earnings guidance to Wall Street—a bold act of ownership that angered analysts but signaled accountability to a bigger picture. He launched the Unilever Sustainable Living Plan, committing to double sales while halving environmental impact and improving livelihoods for millions. He tied executive bonuses to sustainability and social impact metrics, not just financial numbers, and enforced regular reporting and audits on ethical and environmental goals. When executives or divisions fell short, there were real consequences—no excuses.

Within a few years, Unilever's sales grew, profitability strengthened, and its reputation soared as one of the most respected consumer goods companies. Employee morale improved, customers stayed loyal, and the company weathered activist pressures without losing its values. Polman didn't just meet targets—he owned the culture shift that changed the entire organization from "hit the numbers" to "do it right."

Accountability turned teleopathy into trust.

I saw accountability in action when a young Technical Sergeant I worked with caught an airman not following technical procedures while packing an emergency escape parachute. He didn't make a public example out of him or write up the mistake and go on with his day. Instead, he documented the mistake appropriately, took the time to stop what he was doing, retrain the airman on the proper way of performing the task, and helped him learn how to avoid making similar mistakes in the future. His accountability didn't shame—it inspired. Everyone stepped up, knowing their actions mattered.

Engagement: Build a Team That Cares

Engagement means connecting your team to your mission, making them feel valued and heard. It fights teleopathy's detachment by keeping people at the heart of your decisions. Patagonia engages employees by giving them a voice in environmental initiatives, like choosing which causes to fund. That connection fuels loyalty and purpose. I worked with a Commander who engaged his team by leaving his door open so anyone could walk in and share ideas or concerns. One young airman's suggestion identified a critical issue, proving engagement isn't just nice—it's powerful.

Engagement isn't about perks; it's about purpose. When your team feels part of something bigger, they're less likely to cut corners or disconnect. That's how you beat teleopathy's pull.

A Turnaround Story

Let's tie this together with a hypothetical story. Meet Rachel, a plant manager at a manufacturing firm. Her team was struggling—missed deadlines, low morale, and rumors of unethical practices. Rachel saw teleopathy at work: managers fixated on output, rationalizing quality shortcuts, and detached from workers' struggles. She decided to rebuild the culture. She started with transparency, sharing production challenges in weekly updates. She introduced accountability, setting clear ethical standards and rewarding compliance. And she engaged her team, creating a suggestion box that led to worker-led improvements. Within a year, the plant's output doubled, and morale soared. Rachel didn't just fix a problem—she built a culture of integrity.

Your Culture-Building Playbook

Building a culture of integrity starts with you. Here's how to make it happen, Maxwell-style:

> **Lead with Transparency**: Share your decisions openly, even the tough ones. If you make a mistake, own it. Your team will trust you more, not less.

> **Demand Accountability**: Set clear ethical standards and hold everyone to them, starting with yourself. Celebrate those who do right, and correct those who don't.

> **Foster Engagement**: Listen to your team's ideas and concerns. Make them part of your mission, so they feel valued and connected.

During my time in the Air Force, there were several times I needed to transform toxic culture. Units I took over were rife with mistrust, where people hid mistakes to avoid blame. I started weekly staff meetings where my section leaders could share without fear. I spent time with every team, learning their challenges and pooling their ideas for how to resolve them. This culture of integrity turned skeptics into believers, and these units became models of excellence. It wasn't that I was particularly smart or gifted, I simply listened and focused on problem solving, not problem blaming. That's the leader you can be.

Making It Practical

You don't need to run a company like Patagonia to build an ethical culture. Start small: Share one honest update with your team this week. Set one clear ethical rule, like "No shortcuts on quality," and enforce it. Or hold a team meeting to ask, "What's one way we can do better?" These steps plant the seeds for a culture where integrity grows.

Moving Forward

A culture of integrity is your firewall against teleopathy. It's how you ensure your team doesn't just chase goals but lives values. In the chapters ahead, we'll explore the cost of teleopathy, practical decision-making frameworks, and the future of ethical leadership. For now, commit to this: Build a culture where doing right is as natural as breathing. Your team—and your legacy—depend on it.

Pause and Reflect

- What's one thing your workplace does well
  to promote ethics? What needs
  improvement?

- How can you empower your team to speak
  up about ethical concerns?

Leadership Action Steps

1. **Draft an Ethics Charter**: Write a one-page charter outlining your team's commitment to integrity. Have everyone sign it and display it prominently.

2. **Implement Anonymous Feedback**: Set up a system (e.g., a suggestion box or online form) for employees to report ethical concerns without fear.

Chapter 8: The Cost of Teleopathy: Lessons from Failure

Picture a bank that everyone trusted—Wells Fargo, a cornerstone of American finance. In 2016, it was exposed for creating millions of fake accounts to meet aggressive sales targets. Employees, under pressure from leaders fixated on growth, opened unauthorized accounts, forging signatures and betraying customers. The fallout was staggering: $3 billion in fines, a trashed reputation, and a CEO forced to resign. This wasn't just a scandal—it was teleopathy at its worst, where chasing numbers cost trust, money, and integrity. This chapter is about the high price of teleopathy and how you can learn from failure to lead better.

In my Air Force days, I saw failure hit hard. A Staff Sergeant I worked with push to meet a maintenance deadline, disobeyed a direct order from me in order to "get the job done." The results? The young unqualified airman he took with him to do the work, accidently set off an explosive in the parachute, causing damage to the parachute and delaying the mission. He wasn't a bad guy—he was just blinded by teleopathy, fixating on the goal and detaching from reality. That lesson stuck with me and I hope, with him as well: Failure isn't the end; it's a teacher. In Chapter 7, we explored building a culture of integrity to fight teleopathy. Now, we'll look at what happens when teleopathy wins—and how to turn those lessons into leadership wins.

The Price of Teleopathy

Teleopathy isn't just a mistake—it's a wrecking ball. It smashes trust, burns money, and breaks people. When leaders fall into fixation, rationalization, or detachment, as we saw in Chapter 2, the costs pile up: financial losses, ruined reputations, and human suffering. But here's the good news: Every failure is a chance to grow. As John Maxwell says, "Sometimes you win, sometimes you learn." By understanding teleopathy's toll, you can lead with wisdom, avoiding the traps that bring others down.

Think about your own workplace. Have you seen a goal-driven decision backfire? Maybe a rushed project led to errors, or a "win at all costs" mindset hurt morale. Teleopathy's costs aren't just headlines—they're real, and they hit close to home. Let's dive into a failure that shook the world and see what it teaches us.

Wells Fargo: A Failure of Focus

In the early 2010s, Wells Fargo was a banking giant, admired for its customer service. But behind the scenes, teleopathy was brewing. Leaders set sky-high sales goals, pushing employees to open new accounts at all costs. Managers fixated on numbers, rationalizing pressure tactics as "motivating." Employees, fearing job loss, opened 3.5 million fake accounts, forging signatures and deceiving customers. They were detached from the human impact—families charged fees for accounts they didn't want, trust shattered.

When the scandal broke in 2016, the costs were brutal. Wells Fargo paid over $3 billion in fines, faced lawsuits, and saw its stock drop. CEO John Stumpf resigned, and the bank's reputation took years to recover. Employees suffered, too—thousands were fired, many for following orders they felt powerless to resist. This was teleopathy in action: fixation on sales, rationalization of unethical tactics, and detachment from customers' lives. Wells Fargo's leaders didn't set out to fail, but their obsession with goals led them there.

The Ripple Effects

Teleopathy's costs go beyond dollars. Let's break them down:

Financial Costs: Wells Fargo's $3 billion in fines was just the start. They lost customers, faced legal battles, and spent millions on PR to rebuild trust. Enron, from Chapter 1, lost $74 billion and went bankrupt. Teleopathy's price tag is steep.

Reputational Costs: A damaged reputation is hard to fix. Wells Fargo went from trusted to toxic overnight. Customers left, and new ones hesitated. Volkswagen, from Chapter 6, faced similar distrust after its emissions scandal.

When teleopathy erodes trust, it takes years to rebuild.

Human Costs: The real tragedy is the people hurt. Wells Fargo's employees lost jobs or lived in fear, while customers faced financial stress. NASA's *Columbia* disaster, from Chapter 2, cost seven lives. Teleopathy doesn't just hit wallets—it breaks hearts.

These costs show why teleopathy matters. It's not just about one bad decision; it's about the ripple effects that hurts everyone—employees, customers, communities, and you.

Learning from Success: Costco's Contrast

Now, let's look at a company that dodged teleopathy's trap: Costco. While other retailers chased short-term profits, Costco focused on long-term integrity. They pay employees above-average wages, offer generous benefits, and treat suppliers fairly. Leaders like CEO Craig Jelinek avoid fixation by balancing profit with people, rejecting rationalization by being transparent about costs, and staying engaged with employees through open-door policies. The result? Loyal workers, happy customers, and steady growth—Costco's revenue topped $237 billion in 2023, proving ethics pay off.

Costco's leaders show that integrity isn't a sacrifice; it's a strategy. They don't let teleopathy blind them to stakeholders' needs, and their success is a lesson for us all: Lead with values, and the results will follow.

Turning Failure into Growth

Failure is a tough teacher, but it's a great one. Wells Fargo's scandal taught them to rethink their culture. After 2016, they overhauled sales practices, fired unethical leaders, and invested in employee training. By 2023, they'd regained some trust, though the scars remain. The lesson? Failure exposes teleopathy's flaws, but it also opens the door to change. As Maxwell says, "A mistake is only a failure if you don't learn from it."

I saw this in the Air Force. After every unit deployment exercise, our commanders didn't double down on deadlines. They held a "lessons learned" session, where we analyzed what went right and what went wrong—the fixation was on the process and people's concerns not on any specific person. They would then set new protocols, prioritizing safety and teamwork. The next exercise wasn't always perfect, but it was almost always better than the one before it. This was success, not because we worked harder, but because we worked smarter. Failure taught us to lead better. As a leader, my favorite questions to ask were almost always: What did we do right? What did we do wrong? If you were in charge, what would you do differently? You'd be amazed at how well these three simple questions help us fix many issues and develop award winning teams.

Your Leadership Opportunity

Here's where you step in. Teleopathy's costs are a warning, but they're also a chance to grow. Every failure—yours or someone else's—is a lesson in what not to do and how to do better. Think about your workplace. Have you seen teleopathy's price tag—lost trust, wasted money, or hurt feelings? You can change that by learning from failure and leading with integrity.

Let's get practical. To avoid teleopathy's costs, you need to measure the impact of your decisions beyond the bottom line. That means asking, "How does this affect my team, customers, and community?" It means owning mistakes, not hiding them. And it means building a culture, like we discussed in Chapter 7, where ethics trump goals.

A Turnaround Story

Meet Alan Mulally, who became CEO of Ford Motor Company in 2006. The company was in deep trouble—chasing aggressive market-share targets had led to years of rationalizing shortcuts: overproduction of unpopular models, hiding losses in accounting, and a culture where executives fudged forecasts to meet quarterly goals. Teleopathy had taken root—fixation on short-term numbers blinded leaders to long-term damage.

Mulally didn't ignore it. He called a meeting of his top executives and asked each to report their status honestly—green for good, yellow for caution, red for trouble. The first meeting was full of green lights, even though Ford was losing billions. Mulally calmly said, "We're going to lose $17 billion this year. If anyone's business plan is green, they're not being honest." He owned the reality publicly, mortgaged Ford's assets to raise cash (without government bailout), and set clear rules: no more fudging numbers or hiding problems. He introduced weekly Business Plan Review meetings where executives had to report truthfully, with consequences for dishonesty but rewards for transparency and progress.

The first year was brutal—sales dipped, layoffs happened—but trust rebuilt fast. By owning mistakes and tying success to honest reporting, customer focus, and quality rather than just quotas, Ford turned profitable in 2009 and became one of the strongest U.S. automakers. Mulally proved that integrity beats teleopathy—when leaders own actions and enforce accountability, teams shift from "hit the numbers" to "do it right," and results follow.

Making It Practical

You don't need a scandal to learn from failure. Start today with these steps: Review a recent decision that didn't go as planned. Ask, "Did teleopathy play a role?" Share the lesson with your team to build a learning culture. Or create a new metric, like customer feedback or employee morale, to measure the human side of your goals. Small steps like these keep teleopathy's costs at bay and make you a leader others trust.

As I started to climb through the ranks in the Air Force, I was fortunate enough to work in small squadrons which didn't require much leadership ability to keep them successful. That was of course until 1996 when I was put in charge of the 90th fighter squadron, Aircrew Life Support shop, at Elmendorf Air Force Base, Alaska. Although at the time there were only seven of us, this was to be the largest team I had led up to this point in my career. To say the first couple of years were rough would probably be a significant understatement. However, we all have to start somewhere and I certainly did the best I could with the limited leadership tools I had developed up until that point.

Looking back, teleopathy had a hold of me. I was definitely not the kind of leader I, or anyone else, would've enjoyed working for. I didn't have a family and I considered people who did as having some sort of unnecessary distractions from being able to perform their duties. In fact, it wasn't uncommon for us to be working 12 hours a day, and often six days a week. At the time, I didn't see anything wrong with that. Now, I understand. This experience could have broken me but it didn't, instead it transformed me into the leader I am today. The journey wasn't always easy but I assure you…it was worth it.

Moving Forward

Teleopathy's costs are real, but they're not inevitable. By learning from failures like Wells Fargo and successes like Costco, you can lead with wisdom and integrity. In the chapters ahead, we'll explore practical frameworks for ethical decisions and the future of leadership. For now, commit to this: Let failure teach you, not define you. Your leadership can turn lessons into legacies.

Pause and Reflect

- What's a failure you've seen or experienced due to goal obsession? What did you learn?

- How can you turn an ethical mistake into a leadership opportunity?

Leadership Action Steps

1. **Conduct a Failure Analysis**: Review a recent workplace failure (yours or another's). Identify if fixation, rationalization, or detachment played a role, and share one lesson with your team.

2. **Track Hidden Costs**: Create a simple metric (e.g., employee satisfaction, customer trust) to measure the ethical impact of your decisions. Review it monthly.

Chapter 9: A Leader's Toolkit: Frameworks for Ethical Decisions

Let me tell you about Marianne Barner, IKEA's business area manager for carpets and textiles in 1994. IKEA was facing explosive media reports and a major TV documentary exposing child labor in its Indian rug suppliers—young children weaving carpets under exploitative conditions. The company was under intense pressure to keep costs low and maintain supply to meet growth targets, and teleopathy's warning bells were ringing: fixating on price and volume could lead to rationalizing continued use of those suppliers or detaching from the human cost. Instead of ignoring the red flags or quietly cutting ties, Barner applied structured decision-making frameworks. She mapped stakeholders (children and families in India, customers demanding ethical products, suppliers, employees, and IKEA's reputation), assessed long-term risks to the brand and values, and engaged openly with NGOs, suppliers, and internal teams for frank discussions about responsibilities versus short-term savings. She committed to a zero-tolerance policy, launched unannounced audits, partnered with UNICEF and Save the Children to address root causes like poverty and education, and required suppliers to sign legal documents prohibiting child labor with immediate termination for violations. The first years were challenging—supply disruptions and higher costs—but IKEA's reputation strengthened as an ethical leader, customer trust grew, and the company positioned itself as a pioneer in responsible sourcing. Barner didn't just avoid scandal; she used ethical frameworks to beat teleopathy and build lasting integrity.

In my Air Force days, I saw leaders make high-stakes decisions under pressure. One officer I worked with faced a deadline to deploy a new system, the Joint Helmet Mounted Cueing System. The easy choice was to rush it and keep pushing forward, ignoring glitches such as the small cracking that was starting to show up around the mounting mechanism. But he used a clear framework—checking the impact on his team, the mission, and safety standards—before deciding to delay. In my opinion, his choice saved lives and earned trust. That's what this chapter is about: equipping you with practical frameworks to navigate tough calls, avoid teleopathy's traps, and lead with integrity. In Chapter 8, we saw the cost of failure; now, let's build a toolkit to ensure success.

Why You Need a Toolkit

Leadership is like navigating a stormy sea. Teleopathy—fixation, rationalization, detachment—can pull you off course, as we learned in Chapter 2. Without a compass, you're lost. That's where decision-making frameworks come in. They're not just theories; they're tools to keep you grounded when pressure mounts. Whether you're facing a budget cut, a tight deadline, or a moral dilemma, these frameworks help you ask the right questions, weigh the stakes, and choose what's right. As mentioned in a previous chapter, John Maxwell says, "A leader is one who knows the way, goes the way, and shows the way." Your toolkit shows the way when teleopathy threatens to sink you.

Think about your own leadership. When was the last time you faced a tough decision? Did you have a clear process, or did you wing it? A framework isn't a rulebook—it's a guide to make sure your choices align with your values and serve your people. Let's explore three frameworks that will make you a stronger, more ethical leader.

Framework 1: Goodpaster's Three-Step Approach

Professor Goodpaster gives us a powerful framework to fight teleopathy: perspective, frankness, and engagement. Think of it as a three-legged stool—each leg keeps you balanced. Let's break it down with a story.

> **Perspective**: See the big picture—people, values, long-term impact—not just the goal. Imagine a hospital director, Mark, under pressure to cut costs. He could slash staff, but perspective makes him ask, "How will this affect patients and nurses?" He chooses to streamline operations instead, saving money

without hurting care. Perspective fights fixation by zooming out.

Frankness: Tell the truth, even when it's hard. Mark could've rationalized layoffs as "necessary," but he was honest with his board: "Cutting staff hurts our mission." His frankness led to creative solutions, like partnerships with clinics. Frankness stops rationalization in its tracks.

Engagement: Stay connected to your people. Mark walked the hospital floors, listening to nurses' concerns. Their input shaped his plan, keeping morale high. Engagement fights detachment, ensuring your decisions reflect real needs.

I saw this framework in action in the Air Force. My unit faced a tight deadline to prepare for a short notice HHQ Inspection. Instead of rushing (fixation), we checked the impact on the mission, safety and morale (perspective). We admitted the risks to our team (frankness) and involved everyone we believed would be impacted in the solution (engagement). The result? A safe, successful inspection and severely positive remarks. Professor Goodpaster's framework is your first tool—use it to keep teleopathy at bay.

Framework 2: Stakeholder Decision-Making Model

THE PURPOSE-DRIVEN LEADER

The second tool comes from Don Mayer: the stakeholder decision-making model. This says every decision should balance the needs of everyone affected—employees, customers, suppliers, shareholders, and communities. It's like conducting an orchestra, ensuring every section plays in harmony. Let's see it in action.

Consider this hypothetical example: A manufacturing CEO, Lisa, facing pressure to outsource jobs to cut costs. Teleopathy could make her fixate on savings, ignoring workers' livelihoods. Instead, she uses the stakeholder model. She lists her stakeholders: employees (jobs at risk), customers (quality concerns), suppliers (local businesses), and shareholders (profits). She analyzes each group's needs, finding a middle ground: automating some tasks but retraining workers for new roles. The result? Costs drop, jobs stay, and customers get better products. The stakeholder model fights teleopathy by forcing you to consider everyone, not just one goal.

In my Air Force days, I used a version of this model. Facing a budget cut, my team had to decide which programs to keep, which to give away, and which to simply stop doing. We mapped out stakeholders—pilots, mechanics, families—and weighed their needs. By prioritizing safety and readiness, we made cuts that preserved trust and mission success. Not everyone was happy, but in the end, the mission continued and people became accustomed to the changes. This framework is your guide to balanced decisions.

Framework 3: Values-Based Checklist

The third tool is a values-based checklist, blending care, virtue, and duty ethics from Chapter 3. It's a simple list of questions to ensure your decisions align with your values. Here's how it works, tied to a hypothetical story.

Meet Tom, a retailer facing pressure to use a cheap supplier with ethical red flags. He uses this checklist:

> **Care**: "Will this decision harm anyone I'm responsible for, like employees or customers?" Tom sees the supplier's practices could hurt workers and tarnish his brand.

> **Virtue**: "Does this reflect the character I want to model—honesty, fairness, courage?" Tom knows choosing the supplier would compromise his integrity.

> **Duty**: "Is this the right thing to do, based on the golden rule?" Tom wouldn't want his family buying from an unethical source, so he says no.

Tom picks a better supplier, takes a short-term hit, but gains customer loyalty. The checklist kept him grounded. I used a similar approach in the Air Force, asking, "Does this decision care for my team, reflect my values, and do what's right?" It saved me from rushing a project that could've failed.

In the Air Force, we used a similar system. The Air Force Core Values are Integrity, Service, and Excellence. So, oftentimes when I wasn't around and my team was facing a tough decision, I gave them permission to use these three values as their filter to decide if they should or shouldn't do what was being asked of them. This not only empowered them to make decisions on their own, it also freed me (the leader) up to work on higher level issues.

A Case Study: Marianne Barner's Ethical Choice

Let's go back to Marianne Barner, IKEA's business area manager for carpets and textiles in 1994. Her boss and the company faced explosive pressure to keep costs low and maintain supply for growth targets, but a major TV documentary exposed child labor in IKEA's Indian rug suppliers. Teleopathy's warning bells were ringing—fixating on price and volume could mean rationalizing continued use of those suppliers or detaching from the human cost. Instead of ignoring the red flags, Barner used our toolkit.

She applied Professor Goodpaster's framework: perspective showed the supplier's practices could hurt children, families, customers demanding ethical products, and IKEA's reputation; frankness led her to tell leadership the risks openly; engagement meant consulting NGOs, suppliers, and internal teams, who suggested partnering with UNICEF and Save the Children to address root causes like poverty and education. She used the stakeholder model, balancing employee morale, customer trust, supplier relationships, and shareholder needs. And she ran the values-based checklist, confirming the decision aligned with care (protecting vulnerable children), virtue (honesty and courage), and duty (the right thing regardless of short-term cost).

Barner chose to implement a zero-tolerance policy, require legal contracts prohibiting child labor, launch unannounced audits, and invest in education programs for affected families. She took a temporary supply disruption and higher costs, but built a stronger, more trusted brand. IKEA's reputation as an ethical leader grew, customer loyalty strengthened, and the company positioned itself as a pioneer in responsible sourcing. Her toolkit beat teleopathy.

Real-World Inspiration: Starbucks' Turnaround

For inspiration, look at Starbucks. In 2008, they faced criticism for labor practices and sourcing. CEO Howard Schultz didn't rationalize or detach. He used a stakeholder model, engaging farmers to ensure fair trade coffee, being frank about past mistakes, and keeping perspective on customer trust. By 2010, Starbucks' ethical sourcing program

118

boosted its reputation and sales. Schultz's frameworks showed that ethical decisions aren't just right—they're smart.

Making It Practical

Your toolkit is only as good as how you use it. Start today: Pick one framework and apply it to a decision you're facing. Run Professor Goodpaster's three steps—perspective, frankness, engagement—before signing off on a project. List your stakeholders and check how your choice affects them. Or write a values-based checklist and tape it to your desk. These small steps make ethical decisions second nature, keeping teleopathy at bay.

I'll never forget how using this checklist had saved me and my team. During my 30+ years in the Air Force, much of that time we were under immense pressure to cut costs, we all faced tough choices to cut the number of our active-duty service members. This checklist—care for employees, virtue of fairness, duty to do right—led us to make better choices and reshape the Air Force to fit our new reduced budgetary restrictions. Our team stayed intact, and morale soared. That's the power of a toolkit.

Moving Forward

These frameworks—Professor Goodpaster's approach, the stakeholder model, and the values-based checklist—are your tools to lead ethically. In the next chapter, we'll look at the future of ethical leadership and how to stay ahead of teleopathy. For now, commit to this: Pick one tool and use it this week. Your decisions shape your legacy—make them count.

Pause and Reflect

- Which framework feels most actionable for you, and why?

- How can you teach your team to use these tools under pressure?

Leadership Action Steps

1. **Create a Decision-Making Checklist**: Write three questions based on care, virtue, and duty (e.g., "Does this care for my people? Reflect my values? Do what's right?"). Use it for your next big decision.

2. **Practice with Role-Playing**: In your next team meeting, role-play a tough ethical dilemma using one framework. Discuss how it guides your choices.

Chapter 10: The Future of Ethical Leadership

Let me take you to a company that's redefining what it means to lead with purpose. Salesforce, the tech powerhouse behind customer relationship management software, decided years ago to put trust at the heart of its business. Under CEO Marc Benioff, they built a culture where transparent customer relationships and employee empowerment aren't just buzzwords—they're the foundation. Salesforce implemented clear ethical guidelines for data use, ensured fair pricing, and gave employees a voice in shaping company values. By 2023, their revenue hit $31.4 billion, proving that leading with integrity isn't just right—it's a game-changer. Salesforce shows us that the future of leadership belongs to those who beat teleopathy with values. This chapter is about that future—how you can lead ethically in a world where goals can blind us.

In my Air Force days, I saw glimpses of this future. A Staff Sergeant I worked for in the early days of my career with embraced integrity, not just efficiency. He mentored young leaders, such as myself, to prioritize values over metrics, setting a standard that rippled across our unit and throughout my career. His vision showed me that leadership isn't about today's wins—it's about tomorrow's legacy. In Chapter 9, we equipped you with a toolkit for ethical decisions. Now, we'll look ahead, exploring how trends like ethical governance, technology, and education can help you defeat teleopathy and shape a better world.

The Future Is Now

The world is moving fast. Global competition, digital transformation, and rising stakeholder expectations are rewriting the rules of business. But with change comes opportunity. Teleopathy—fixation, rationalization, detachment—thrives when leaders chase short-term goals over long-term values, as we saw in Chapter 2. The future of leadership belongs to those who embrace new tools, new mindsets, and new priorities to keep ethics first. As John Maxwell says, "Change is inevitable. Growth is optional." You can choose to grow as an ethical leader, using tomorrow's trends to fight teleopathy today.

Think about your workplace. Are you ready for what's coming? Customers demand honesty, employees want purpose, and society expects accountability. The future isn't just about hitting targets—it's about hitting the right ones. Let's explore three trends that will shape ethical leadership and how you can use them to stay ahead of teleopathy.

Trend 1: Ethical Governance—Leading with Transparency

Ethical governance is about building systems that prioritize transparency and accountability in every decision. It's not about checking boxes—it's about ensuring your organization lives its values. Salesforce is a prime example. They adopted strict policies for data privacy, openly sharing how customer information is used, and set clear standards for fair pricing. They held leaders accountable through regular audits and gave employees a say in ethical guidelines. These moves fought teleopathy's fixation on revenue by keeping trust first. By 2023, Salesforce's market value topped $250 billion, showing that ethical governance isn't just right—it's a competitive edge.

Ethical governance forces you to think beyond profits. Instead of obsessing over sales, you build systems that ensure integrity, like transparent reporting or ethical audits. In the Air Force, I saw a commander do this by setting up open forums where every decision was explained, earning trust and boosting morale. Ethical governance is your chance to lead with clarity, keeping teleopathy at bay.

Trend 2: Technology as an Ethical Amplifier

Technology is transforming leadership, and it's a game-changer for ethics. In Chapter 5, we saw how blogs, podcasts, and videos spread ethical ideas. The future goes further. Imagine virtual reality (VR) training where your team faces ethical dilemmas in a simulated boardroom, practicing how to resist teleopathy's pull. Or AI tools that flag decisions at risk of fixation, like a sales target that compromises client trust. Salesforce leads here, with AI-driven tools that ensure ethical data use, like flagging potential privacy breaches before they happen.

I saw technology's power in the Air Force. We used digital dashboards to track mission metrics, catching risks before they became crises. One dashboard flagged a rushed training process, letting us pause and avoid a potential failure. Technology didn't just help us work—it helped us work right. As a leader, you can use technology to amplify ethics, from apps that track compliance to platforms that let employees report concerns anonymously. The future is digital, and it's yours to shape.

Trend 3: Education for Ethical Leaders

The future needs leaders who think ethically, and that starts with education. Business schools like Wharton are expanding ethics courses, teaching students to spot teleopathy's symptoms. Executive programs are evolving, too, with workshops on stakeholder-focused leadership. But education isn't just for MBAs—it's for every leader. Salesforce trains employees at all levels on ethical decision-making, ensuring everyone understands the company's commitment to trust. This fights teleopathy by building a workforce that thinks before acting.

In my Air Force days, we had ethics training, but one leader made it stick. He used real stories— calling out and recognizing people who were doing things right—to show why values matter. That training shaped how I lead today. You can do the same, mentoring your team or pushing for ethics in your industry. Education builds leaders who see through teleopathy's fog.

A Case Study: Turning Vision into Reality

Let's tie this together with a hypothetical story. Meet Elena, a startup founder in 2025. Her fintech company was growing fast, but teleopathy was creeping in—sales teams chased deals with risky clients, fixating on growth. Elena saw the future and acted. She embraced ethical governance, setting transparent contract standards and holding regular ethics audits. She used technology, launching an AI tool to flag unethical deals and a VR platform for ethics training. And she invested in education, mentoring her team on care, virtue, and duty from Chapter 3. The result? Her startup became a leader in ethical fintech, earning trust and talent.

Elena's story shows how to use these trends. She didn't just react to change—she shaped it, beating teleopathy by leading with purpose. You can do the same, whether you're running a startup or a small team.

Real-World Inspiration: Salesforce's Legacy

Salesforce's journey is your blueprint. Marc Benioff's leadership shows that ethical governance, technology, and education can defeat teleopathy. They used AI to ensure ethical data practices, trained employees on trust-based decision-making, and set governance standards that kept values first. When faced with pressure to prioritize revenue, they doubled down on purpose, like ensuring fair pricing for clients. Salesforce's growth—$31.4 billion in revenue by 2023—proves that ethical leadership isn't a sacrifice; it's a strength.

Your Leadership Moment

The future of ethical leadership starts with you. You don't need to run a tech giant to make a difference. Embrace ethical governance by setting one transparent policy, like open reporting. Use technology to share an ethical story or train your people. Mentor a colleague on integrity, passing the torch. These trends—ethical governance, technology, education—are your tools to fight teleopathy and build a legacy.

I'll never forget the leader who shaped the future for me. He walked into our shop and looked past all the failed programs, unhappy people and spotted me, doing the best with the leadership skills I had (which wasn't a lot, a three-day leadership course over ten years earlier in my career). He pulled me aside, mentored me and shaped me into the leader I am today. If I accomplished anything at all in my career, it's because he demonstrated integrity and I followed his example. That's the leader you can be.

Making It Practical

Start today. Set a goal to improve transparency, like sharing one honest update with your team. Create a short video sharing an ethical lesson, or use a free app to track team feedback. Mentor one person this week on what integrity means to you. These steps don't just fight teleopathy—they shape a future where ethics lead the way.

Moving Forward

The future is yours to build. By embracing ethical governance, technology, and education, you can lead with integrity and inspire others to do the same. These trends set the stage for addressing polarization in Ch. 11, where ethics meets today's divides. For now, commit to this: Be the leader who shapes tomorrow with ethics today.

Pause and Reflect

- What's one change you want to see in your industry's approach to ethics?

- How will you inspire the next generation of leaders to avoid teleopathy?

Leadership Action Steps

1. **Mentor a Young Leader**: Share one lesson from this book with a colleague or mentee, focusing on how to prioritize ethics over goals.

2. **Advocate for Ethics Training**: Push for a workshop or course on ethical governance or leadership in your organization or industry.

Chapter 11: Teleopathy in the Age of Polarization

I've seen it in the Air Force more times than I can count: a policy rolled out with the best of intentions, meant to build unity or boost performance, but ending up dividing the team or creating resentment. One time, leadership pushed a "team-building" program that mandated group sessions on resiliency. The idea was solid—get everyone on the same page about looking out for each other, respect and working together. But it was implemented with a heavy hand, like a box to check rather than a genuine conversation. Some Airmen felt it was forced politics, others thought it ignored the real issues on the ground like manpower and resource shortages. Morale dipped, arguments flared, and the mission suffered. Good intent, negative consequences.

Over the past five years, I've seen the same thing in corporations with initiatives like Diversity, Equity, and Inclusion (DEI) and Environmental, Social, and Governance (ESG) standards. What started as pushes for fairness and responsibility have often turned into polarizing forces, with backlash, lawsuits, and retreats (companies scaling back, abandoning, or publicly distancing themselves from these programs). This is teleopathy amplified by politics: when hyper-partisanship becomes a stand-in for true conscience, it leads to outsourcing moral insight to ideologies instead of building real common ground. This chapter explores how political views pushed into corporations create unintended divisions, and how we can reclaim balance using the lessons we've discussed.

The Trap of Partisan Goals: Symptoms in Action

Teleopathy doesn't change just because the goal is "social good." In the age of polarization, it shows up when corporations adopt political agendas like DEI or ESG without balance. The symptoms are the same as always:

Fixation: Leaders fixate on DEI metrics—hiring quotas, training hours, or diversity scores—or ESG targets like carbon reduction numbers—turning them into the only measure of success. Everything else, like merit, team cohesion, or business results, gets sidelined.

Rationalization: When pushback comes, it's rationalized away as "resistance to change," "it's for the greater good" or "privilege." Corporations start acting like political entities, justifying partisan decisions as ethical necessities.

Detachment: Leaders detach from the human impact—employees who feel reverse discriminated in DEI efforts, teams divided by ESG mandates that feel forced, or customers alienated by perceived virtue-signaling. The focus on "the greater good" ignores the real harm on the ground.

Think of it like that resiliency program I mentioned: the goal was to support and unity, but fixation on the agenda detached leaders from the Airmen's daily realities, leading to division. In corporations, DEI and ESG have followed a similar path. What began as responses to genuine inequities and environmental concerns have often become teleopathic obsessions, with companies like Disney, Exxon, or Anheuser-Busch facing lawsuits and retreats because the implementation lost balance.

Goodpaster's Insights: Counterfeits and Moral Common Ground

Professor Goodpaster's recent reflections give us the tools to understand this. He warns about "counterfeits" for conscience—things like hyper-partisanship that masquerade as moral progress but actually erode it. When corporations "outsource" their ethical thinking to political ideologies, they lose sight of their role as human institutions serving the common good. DEI and ESG can become such counterfeits when they're pushed as partisan agendas rather than shared values.

He deepens this with the idea of "institutional insight"—leaders must see corporations as part of society's moral fabric, fostering awareness of individual and collective good. He calls for "moral common ground," where initiatives like DEI and ESG could potentially unite rather than divide. Without this, teleopathy takes over: fixation on political goals detaches the organization from broader human dignity.

Goodpaster expands this to sustainability, a key part of ESG, as a core obligation for corporations. He describes it as a "fiduciary" duty to the natural environment, tied to the provision of goods and services. Corporations aren't just profit machines—they have responsibilities to future generations, balancing resource use with moral accountability. But when ESG becomes a teleopathic obsession—fixating on environmental metrics like carbon footprints without considering economic realities or stakeholder buy-in—it turns into a counterfeit. Leaders rationalize extreme measures, detaching from employees who bear the costs or communities that rely on the business. Goodpaster's point is clear: sustainability succeeds when grounded in conscience and common ground, not when it's outsourced to partisan politics or unbalanced goals.

From my view as a Chief, this resonates. In the Air Force, we built unity through shared values, purpose, mission, and respect, not mandated ideologies. Goodpaster's insights show why corporate DEI and ESG often fail—it's teleopathy in disguise, prioritizing politics over people.

A Real-World Example: The DEI Backlash

Let's look at a true case: Disney's experience from 2020 to 2023. Under then-CEO Bob Chapek, Disney aggressively pushed DEI initiatives, including public stances on political issues like Florida's Parental Rights in Education Act. The intent was positive—promote inclusion and support underrepresented groups. But it became teleopathic: fixation on the agenda led to rationalization of overreach, like mandatory diversity trainings and content changes that some employees and customers saw as forced or even brainwashing. Detachment from stakeholders showed when internal dissent was dismissed, and external backlash (lawsuits, boycotts, stock drops) was blamed on "culture wars."

The consequences were real: employee morale suffered, with reports of division; customer trust eroded, leading to financial losses; and shareholders pushed back, resulting in Chapek's ouster. Bob Iger's return in 2023 was meant to refocus on entertainment over activism, echoing the need for moral common ground—balance politics with the common good to avoid teleopathy's pitfalls. However, it wouldn't appear at the time of this writing that he has been successful in any of those initiatives and the company's future is still in question.

A second example shows how this plays out in marketing: Anheuser-Busch's 2023 Bud Light campaign featuring transgender influencer Dylan Mulvaney. The intent was to promote inclusivity and appeal to a younger, diverse audience as part of broader DEI efforts. But it became a teleopathic misstep: fixation on the social agenda rationalized the ad without fully engaging or considering the brand's core customer base, leading to detachment from loyal consumers who felt alienated or unappreciated. The backlash was massive—boycotts, sales drops of over 25%, and billions in lost market value. Critics accused the company of pushing politics over product, and the CEO's initial response downplayed the impact, further fueling division. This case, like Disney's, highlights how DEI-driven decisions can create unintended consequences when they lose balance and moral common ground.

A third example illustrates the ESG side: Exxon's experience from 2021 onward. Under CEO Darren Woods, ExxonMobil faced intense pressure from investors, political leaders, and environmental activists to adopt aggressive ESG targets, including rapid carbon reductions and net-zero commitments. The intent was positive—address climate change and improve corporate responsibility. But it became teleopathic for some stakeholders: fixation on ESG metrics rationalized massive shifts in strategy without fully considering the energy industry's realities, leading to detachment from customers, employees, suppliers, and shareholders who prioritized energy security, reliability, and profits. The backlash was fierce—investor revolts, with groups like Engine No. 1 successfully electing board members in 2021 to push back against what they saw as overzealous ESG agendas. Lawsuits followed, accusing the company of misleading on climate risks, and stock volatility increased as the push for ESG clashed with operational needs. Exxon responded by balancing with investments in low-carbon tech while defending fossil fuels, but the episode showed how ESG can divide when detached from business fundamentals and moral common ground.

Similar issues have played out with ESG, where companies like BlackRock faced criticism for pushing environmental mandates that detached from shareholder priorities, leading to investor pullbacks. In fact, there seems to be no shortage of examples where ESG has been destroying companies, even entire industries, that are critical to our modern-day society. However, there are very limited examples of where it has actually done any good. Which should make everyone wonder, is ESG even needed at all or was it an unnecessary teleopathic response from the beginning?

Your Take: Lessons from the Flightline

As a Chief Master Sergeant, I learned that unity isn't mandated—it's earned through shared values, purpose, mission, and respect. DEI and ESG in corporations fail when they become teleopathic goals, detached from the team's daily reality. The insights here explain why: politics isn't conscience. In my coaching, I've seen leaders succeed by asking key questions—"Does this initiative serve our common good, or is it partisan outsourcing?" From the flightline to the boardroom, the answer is to find or create harmony: use DEI and ESG to build real inclusion and responsibility, not divide.

Applying the Frameworks: Tools to Reclaim Harmony

To beat polarization-driven teleopathy, use the book's tools with these insights:

Goodpaster's Three-Step Framework (adapted for DEI and ESG):

Perspective: List stakeholders (employees of all views, customers, community). What long-term impacts could a DEI or ESG policy have? (e.g., "Quotas might boost diversity but hurt merit-based morale; green targets could reduce emissions but strain operations.")

Frankness: Write an honest statement about risks. (e.g., "This could be seen as partisan, dividing the team.")

Engagement: Involve everyone—hold anonymous surveys to find moral common ground.

Stakeholder Model: Balance DEI and ESG goals with all needs—e.g., equity for underrepresented groups without alienating

others, or sustainability without ignoring
financial realities.

Leadership Action Steps

Values-Based Checklist:

Care: Does this help or harm team unity?

Virtue: Is it honest and fair?

Duty: Does it serve the common good?

Exercise: DEI/ESG Dilemma Role-Play

- Goal: Practice balancing political initiatives.

- Steps: Present a scenario (e.g., "Mandate DEI training or ESG reporting—will it unite or divide?"). Use the adapted framework to discuss. Reflect: "How can we find moral common ground?"

The Future of Ethical Leadership

The call for moral common ground is the way forward: corporations aren't political battlegrounds. Teleopathy thrives in polarization, but leaders like you can break it by protecting conscience from partisanship. From my flightline days, I know: focus on shared purpose, values, and mission, not mandates. Lead with purpose, use these tools, and you'll build teams that thrive—ethically and effectively. In the Conclusion, we'll tie together everything you've learned, challenging you to create a lasting legacy. The cycle ends with you.

Conclusion: Lead with Integrity, Win with Purpose

Let me tell you about a leader who changed everything. In 2006, Indra Nooyi became CEO of PepsiCo at a time when the company was heavily focused on aggressive quarterly sales and profit targets. The pressure to deliver short-term results had led to rationalization of unhealthy products, environmental shortcuts, and detachment from broader stakeholder needs. Teleopathy had taken hold—fixation on numbers over purpose. But Nooyi refused to let it win. She publicly declared a new direction: "Performance with Purpose," committing PepsiCo to double revenue while reducing environmental impact and improving health outcomes for consumers. She owned the shift, engaged employees and stakeholders in frank conversations, and used decision frameworks to balance shareholder demands with employee well-being, customer health, and community impact. She tied executive incentives to sustainability and diversity goals, reformed product portfolios, and invested in ethical sourcing. The early years were tough—stock dipped, critics pushed back—but by the time she stepped down in 2018, PepsiCo's revenue had grown significantly, its reputation as a responsible leader strengthened, and it became a model for purpose-driven business. Nooyi didn't just meet targets; she built a legacy of integrity that proved ethical leadership beats teleopathy..

That's what this book is about: helping you become a leader like Indra Nooyi, one who beats teleopathy and leads with purpose. We've traveled a long road together—10 chapters packed with stories, tools, and lessons to navigate the ethical challenges of a goal-obsessed world. In my Air Force days, I learned that leadership isn't about hitting every target; it's about hitting the right ones, the ones that make your team, your organization, and the world better. Now, it's time to tie it all together and challenge you to lead with integrity, starting today.

The Danger of Teleopathy

Teleopathy, as we learned in Chapter 1, is the unbalanced pursuit of goals that blinds you to ethics. It's the trap that snared Enron, collapsing under $74 billion in losses when leaders fixated on wealth (Chapter 1). It's what drove NASA's *Columbia* disaster, costing seven lives because of a "keep-it-flying" obsession (Chapter 2). It's what led Volkswagen to cheat emissions tests, paying $18 billion in fines (Chapter 6), and Wells Fargo to create 3.5 million fake accounts, costing $3 billion and their reputation (Chapter 8). These stories aren't just headlines—they're warnings. Teleopathy's symptoms—fixation, rationalization, detachment—can destroy trust, money, and lives if you let them.

But you don't have to. This book has shown you how to spot teleopathy's red flags (Chapter 2), use ethical frameworks like care, virtue, and duty to stay grounded (Chapter 3), and navigate global challenges with respect and integrity (Chapter 4). We've explored technology as a tool to spread ethical ideas (Chapter 5), the leader's role in setting the tone (Chapter 6), and building a culture where integrity thrives (Chapter 7). We've learned from failure's costs (Chapter 8), equipped you with decision-making frameworks (Chapter 9), and looked to the future with trends like ethical governance and education (Chapter 10). Each chapter is a piece of your leadership puzzle, helping you avoid teleopathy's traps and lead with purpose.

Key Lessons from the Journey

Let's pull it together with lessons from the stories we've shared:

- **Enron (Chapter 1)**: Fixation on profits without a moral compass leads to ruin. Lead with stakeholder balance, not goal obsession.
- **NASA (Chapter 2)**: Ignoring warnings for the sake of deadlines costs lives. Perspective, frankness, and engagement keep you grounded.
- **Nike (Chapter 4)**: Global leadership demands respect for cultural values without compromising ethics. Pluralistic ethics, as Robert Audi suggests, finds the balance.
- **Salesforce (Chapter 10)**: Ethical leadership isn't a sacrifice—it's a strength. Their focus on trust and transparency drove $31.4 billion in revenue.

- **Patagonia (Chapter 7)**: A culture of integrity, built on transparency and engagement, beats teleopathy and builds loyalty.
- **Wells Fargo (Chapter 8)**: Failure teaches hard lessons. Learn from mistakes to rebuild trust and avoid teleopathy's costs.

These stories show that teleopathy is a choice—you can fall into it, or you can rise above it. Leaders like Indra Nooyi, who turned her company around, or Salesforce's Marc Benioff, who built trust through ethical practices, chose to rise. You can, too.

Your Call to Action

This book isn't just a read—it's a challenge. Teleopathy is everywhere, tempting you to chase goals over values. But you're not just any leader. You're someone who can change the game, who can build a workplace where integrity wins. Remember the words of John Maxwell, "Leadership is influence—nothing more, nothing less." Your influence starts now. Here's your call to action:

- **Spot Teleopathy**: Watch for fixation, rationalization, and detachment in your decisions. Use the symptom checklist from Chapter 2 to stay alert.
- **Use Your Toolkit**: Apply the frameworks from Chapter 9—Professor Goodpaster's perspective, frankness, and engagement; the

stakeholder model; the values-based checklist—to make ethical choices.

- **Build a Culture**: Follow Chapter 7's pillars—transparency, accountability, engagement—to create a workplace where ethics thrive.
- **Shape the Future**: Embrace ethical governance, technology, and education from Chapter 10 to lead with purpose, not just profit.

I'll never forget my career in the Air Force, moving from base to base fixing programs. I'd take over a team riddled with ethical lapses—workers hiding defects to meet quotas. I wouldn't just fix the problem; I'd do all I could to transform the culture. I used technology to share stories of integrity, mentored my teams on ethical frameworks, and set clear values. My teams didn't just meet goals—they exceeded them, with trust as their foundation. That's the legacy you can build.

Your Leadership Legacy

Leadership isn't about what you achieve today—it's about what you leave behind. Will your team remember you as someone who chased numbers or someone who changed lives? Teleopathy tempts you to choose the former, but you can choose the latter. Start with one decision this week. Use a framework from Chapter 9 to guide it. Share a story of integrity with your team, like we explored in Chapter 5. Mentor someone, as we discussed in

Chapter 10. These small steps build a legacy that outlasts any target.

In the Air Force, I saw leaders leave different legacies. Some chased deadlines and lost trust; others prioritized values and built a team that thrived. The difference? The second set of leaders saw every decision as a chance to lead with integrity. That's your chance, too. Write your legacy as an ethical leader, starting today.

Pause and Reflect

- What's one action you'll take this week to combat teleopathy in your workplace?

- How will you measure your success as an ethical leader?

Leadership Action Steps

1. **Create a Personal Ethics Pledge**: Write a one-sentence commitment to lead with integrity (e.g., "I will make every decision with care, virtue, and duty"). Review it monthly to stay on track.

2. **Start a Workplace Book Club**: Share this book with your team and discuss one chapter a month, focusing on how to apply its lessons to your workplace.

Appendix A: Glossary of Key Terms

Words matter, especially when you're navigating the tricky waters of ethical leadership. This glossary defines the key terms we've used throughout this book to help you fight teleopathy and lead with integrity. Keep it handy as a quick reference for your leadership journey.

- **Care Ethics**: An ethical framework that emphasizes relationships and empathy, prioritizing the well-being of those you serve—your team, customers, and community. It fights teleopathy's detachment by keeping people first (Chapter 3).
- **Detachment**: A symptom of teleopathy where leaders disconnect from the human impact of their decisions, treating people like numbers (Chapter 2).
- **Duty Theory**: An ethical framework based on doing what's right because it aligns with universal principles, like the golden rule: treat others as you'd want to be treated (Chapter 3).
- **Ethical Governance**: Systems and policies that ensure transparency and accountability in decision-making, keeping values first and fighting teleopathy's fixation (Chapter 10).
- **Fixation**: A symptom of teleopathy where leaders obsess over a single goal, like profit

or deadlines, ignoring broader consequences (Chapter 2).

- **Moral Institutionalism**: The practice of imposing universal (often Western) ethical standards on different cultures, which can lead to unintended harm if not balanced with local values (Chapter 4).
- **Pluralistic Ethics**: An approach to global leadership that respects cultural differences while upholding core ethical principles, avoiding teleopathy's rationalization (Chapter 4).
- **Rationalization**: A symptom of teleopathy where leaders justify unethical actions as "necessary" to achieve a goal (Chapter 2).
- **Stakeholder-Focused Leadership**: A leadership approach that considers the needs of all groups affected by a decision— employees, customers, suppliers, shareholders, and communities—to avoid teleopathy's narrow focus (Chapter 1, Chapter 9).
- **Teleopathy**: The unbalanced pursuit of goals that blinds leaders to ethical considerations, leading to fixation, rationalization, and detachment (Chapter 1).
- **Virtue Theory**: An ethical framework focused on building character traits like honesty, courage, and fairness, helping leaders avoid teleopathy's rationalization (Chapter 3).

Appendix B: Resources for Ethical Leadership

Great leaders never stop learning. Below is a curated list of books, articles, podcasts, and tools to deepen your understanding of ethical leadership and keep teleopathy at bay. These resources build on the ideas in this book, offering practical insights for your journey.

Books

- **Maxwell, J. C. (1998).** *The 21 Irrefutable Laws of Leadership.* **Nashville, TN: Thomas Nelson.**
  - o Why read it? Maxwell's timeless principles inspire leaders to influence with integrity, aligning with our focus on setting an ethical tone (Chapter 6).
- **Brown, B. (2018).** *Dare to Lead: Brave Work. Tough Conversations. Whole Hearts.* **New York, NY: Random House.**
  - o Why read it? Brown's focus on courage and vulnerability complements our engagement strategies to fight detachment (Chapter 7).
- **Goodpaster, K. E. (2010).** *Conscience and Corporate Culture.* **Malden, MA: Blackwell Publishing.**

- o Why read it? Goodpaster's work on teleopathy and ethical decision-making underpins our frameworks (Chapters 2, 9).
- **Goodpaster, K. E. (2022). Times of Insight: Conscience, Corporations, and the Common Good. Springer.**
  - o Why read it? Goodpaster's newest work ties Teleopathy to channelized attention and provides deeper insights on polarization in corporations (Chapter 4, 7).
- **Lightner, M. T. (2023). The Untouchable Way: Living Your Life Exempt From Criticism or Control. Dare2Dream LD.**
  - o Why read it? Lightner's work on values helps leaders identify and establish values for themselves and their organizations (Parts I, II, and III).

Articles and Blogs

- **Hoban, J. (2012, January 2). *What Are Values, Morals, and Ethics?* [Web log post]. Retrieved from http://managementhelp.org/blogs/business-ethics/2012/01/02/what-are-values-morals-and-ethics/**
  - o Why read it? This blog, cited in Chapter 5, offers a clear breakdown of ethics, useful for teaching teams about values.

- **Audi, R. (2009). Objectivity Without Egoism: Toward Balance in Business Ethics.** *Academy of Management Learning & Education, 8(2), 263–274.* **doi:10.5465/AMLE.2009.41788850**
  - Why read it? Audi's pluralistic ethics, discussed in Chapter 4, helps leaders navigate global challenges with balance.

Podcasts and Videos

- **Bromell, T. (Producer). (n.d.).** *Acting With Integrity Introduction* **[Video podcast]. Retrieved from http://www.icaew.com/en/technical/ethics/ethics-media/ethics-audio-updates**
  - Why watch it? This podcast, featured in Chapter 5, shares real stories of integrity, perfect for sparking team discussions.
- **Busam, L., Dickson, B., Doster, A., & Rod, K. (2009, June 22).** *Business Ethics Through Film: Monsters Inc.* **[Video]. Retrieved from https://www.youtube.com/watch?v=CUCSK1QFwts**
  - Why watch it? This student-made video, cited in Chapter 5, uses pop culture to teach ethics in an engaging way.

Tools

- **Stakeholder Mapping Template**: Create a chart listing all stakeholders (employees, customers, suppliers, etc.) and their needs. Use it to apply the stakeholder model from Chapter 9.
- **Ethics Decision Checklist**: A one-page list of questions based on care, virtue, and duty ethics (Chapter 9). Example: "Does this decision care for my people? Reflect my values? Do what's right?"
- **Anonymous Feedback Platform**: Use tools like SurveyMonkey or Google Forms to let employees report ethical concerns safely, supporting engagement (Chapter 7).

Appendix C: Templates for Ethical Decision-Making

These templates are practical tools to help you apply the frameworks from Chapter 9. Use them to make ethical decisions and keep teleopathy at bay. They're simple, actionable, and ready to adapt to your workplace.

Template 1: Professor Goodpaster's Three-Step Framework

Use this to ensure perspective, frankness, and engagement guide your decisions.

1. **Perspective**: List all stakeholders affected by your decision. What are the short- and long-term impacts on them? (e.g., "Cutting costs could save money but hurt employee morale.")
2. **Frankness**: Write one honest statement about the ethical risks of your decision. (e.g., "Rushing this project might compromise quality.")
3. **Engagement**: Identify one way to involve your team or stakeholders in the decision. (e.g., "Hold a team meeting to discuss concerns.")

Template 2: Stakeholder Decision-Making Model

Use this to balance stakeholder needs, as outlined in Chapter 9.

1. **Identify Stakeholders**: List all groups affected (e.g., employees, customers, suppliers, shareholders, community).
2. **Assess Needs**: For each stakeholder, write one key need or concern (e.g., "Employees need job security; customers need quality.")
3. **Balance Solutions**: Brainstorm one solution that addresses all needs. (e.g., "Automate tasks but retrain employees to maintain jobs.")

Template 3: Values-Based Checklist

Use this to align decisions with care, virtue, and duty ethics (Chapter 3).

- **Care**: Will this decision harm or help those I'm responsible for? (e.g., "Will this supplier choice affect worker safety?")
- **Virtue**: Does this reflect the character I want to model (honesty, fairness, courage)? (e.g., "Am I being transparent with my team?")
- **Duty**: Is this the right thing to do, based on the golden rule? (e.g., "Would I want this decision made for me?")

Template 4: Ethics Charter

Use this to create a team commitment to integrity, as suggested in Chapter 7.

- **Purpose**: Write a one-sentence mission for your team's ethical culture. (e.g., "We commit to transparency, accountability, and respect in all we do.")
- **Values**: List three core values (e.g., honesty, fairness, collaboration).
- **Pledge**: Have team members sign a pledge to uphold these values. (e.g., "I will make decisions that reflect our values and report concerns openly.")

Appendix D: Reflective Exercises

These exercises are designed to spark creative thinking and help you apply the book's lessons, as outlined in your request. Use them alone or with your team to deepen your commitment to ethical leadership.

Exercise 1: Teleopathy Symptom Check

- **Goal**: Spot teleopathy's symptoms (Chapter 2).
- **Steps**: Reflect on a recent decision. Ask: Did I fixate on one goal? Rationalize a shortcut? Detach from stakeholders? Write down one way to avoid these in the future.
- **Example**: "I fixated on a deadline and ignored team burnout. Next time, I'll check in with my team first."

Exercise 2: Stakeholder Mapping

- **Goal**: Apply the stakeholder model (Chapter 9).
- **Steps**: Pick an upcoming decision. List all stakeholders and their needs. Brainstorm one solution that balances them. Share with a colleague for feedback.
- **Example**: "For a cost-cutting decision, I listed employees (job security), customers (quality), and shareholders (profits).

Solution: Streamline processes but maintain staff."

Exercise 3: Ethical Dilemma Role-Play

- **Goal**: Practice ethical decision-making (Chapter 9).
- **Steps**: In a team meeting, present a hypothetical dilemma (e.g., "Should we use a cheaper supplier with ethical risks?"). Use one framework from Chapter 9 to discuss and resolve it. Reflect on what you learned.
- **Example**: "We used the values-based checklist and decided against the supplier, prioritizing duty."

Exercise 4: DEI/ESG Dilemma Role-Play

- **Goal:** Practice balancing political initiatives.
- **Steps:** Present a scenario (e.g., "Mandate DEI training or ESG reporting—will it unite or divide?"). Use the adapted framework to discuss. Reflect: "How can we find moral common ground?"
- **Example:** "We used the adapted Goodpaster's framework to discuss a DEI training mandate and decided to make it voluntary with input sessions, finding moral common ground to avoid division."

SPECIAL THANKS!

I would like to say **THANK YOU** to some special people who really helped me with this book:

Angie Lightner

Lisa Hoffman

Professor Kenneth Goodpaster

ABOUT THE AUTHOR

"When you truly believe in yourself and what you are trying to accomplish, others will believe in you and your vision as well."

~ Mike T. Lightner

Mike Lightner is a retired Chief Master Sergeant from the United States Air Force with extensive knowledge and experience in team leadership and personnel development. In his last position, as the Aircrew Flight Equipment Career Field Manager, he oversaw the leadership, growth, development, and management of over 5,200 Total Force (Active Duty, Air National Guard, and Reserve Airmen, and civilian employees) worldwide. Additionally, Mike was responsible for the inspection, maintenance, acquisition, and sustainment of over $8 Billion in critical life sustaining aircrew and passenger safety, survival, and chemical defense equipment.

As a John C. Maxwell Certified International Coach, Teacher, and Speaker, Mike offers workshops, seminars, keynote speaking, and coaching, designed to aid you in your personal and professional growth through study and practical application of proven leadership methods.

Mike's passion is to develop leaders who, in turn, have a passion to develop leaders. If this is the type culture you would like to create within your organization, he stands ready to help you achieve your goal!

mikelightner@d2dleadership.com

www.d2dleadership.com

OTHER BOOKS BY MIKE

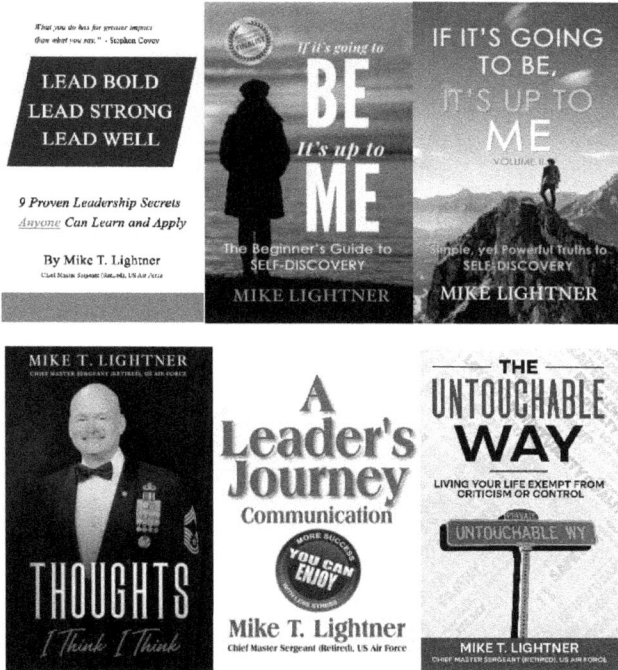

Available on Amazon

* 9 7 9 8 9 9 3 2 6 0 3 0 3 *